Working and learning together for change

Edited by
Colin Biott and Jennifer Nias

Open University Press
Buckingham • Philadelphia

This book is dedicated, with gratitude and respect, to all the teachers with whom we have worked and learned and who have helped us to change.

Open University Press
Celtic Court
22 Ballmoor
Buckingham
MK18 1XW

and
1900 Frost Road, Suite 101
Bristol, PA 19007, USA

First Published 1992

A catalogue record of this book is available from the British Library

Library of Congress Cataloging-in-Publication Data

Working and learning together for change/edited by Colin Biott and
    Jennifer Nias.
        p.   cm. – (Developing teachers and teaching)
    Includes bibliographical references (p.   ) and index.
    ISBN 0-335-09716-2
    1. Teachers – In-service training – Great Britain.   2. Team learning
approach in education – Great Britain.   I. Biott, Colin.   II. Nias,
Jennifer.   III. Series.
    LB1731.W6   1992
    371.1′46′0941 – dc20   91-33756
                                                                CIP

Typeset by Graphicraft Typesetters Co. Ltd.
Printed in Great Britain by St Edmundsbury Press Ltd.,
Bury St Edmunds, Suffolk

Working and learning
together for change

Developing Teachers and Teaching

Series Editor: **Christopher Day**, Reader in Education Management and Director of Advanced Post-Graduate Courses in the School of Education, University of Nottingham.

Teachers and schools will wish not only to survive but also to flourish in a period which holds increased opportunities for self-management – albeit within centrally designed guidelines – combined with increased public and professional accountability. Each of the authors in this series provides perspectives which will both challenge and support practitioners at all levels who wish to extend their critical skills, qualities and knowledge of schools, pupils and teachers.

Current titles:

Angela Anning: *The First Years at School*

Les Bell and Chris Day (eds): *Managing the Professional Development of Teachers*

Colin Biott and Jennifer Nias (eds): *Working and Learning Together for Change*

Joan Dean: *Professional Development in School*

C. T. Patrick Diamond: *Teacher Education as Transformation*

John Elliott: *Action Research for Educational Change*

John Olson: *Understanding Teaching*

John Smyth: *Teachers as Collaborative Learners*

Contents

Series editor's introduction   vii
Notes on contributors   ix
Acknowledgements   xi

Introduction
Jennifer Nias   xiv

Part I   Working together to help others change   1

1   Imposed support for teachers' learning: implementation or
    development partnerships?
    Colin Biott   3
2   Preparing for school staff membership: students in primary
    teacher education
    Robin Yeomans   19
3   Working together: developing reflective student teachers
    Kate Ashcroft   33

Part II   The subjective experience of changing with others   47

4   Reflections on a head and deputy partnership
    Penelope A. Campbell   49
5   In search of authenticity: learning to be a headteacher
    Sheena Ball   62
6   Working together: being a member of a teachers' group
    Mary Heath   79

7   Learning to help others
     Jay Mawdsley   86
8   Insight, direction and support: a case study of collaborative
     enquiry in classroom research
     Andy Convery   91

**Part III Feminist perspectives on working and
            learning together**   107

9   Learning brings us together: the meaning of feminist adult
     education
     Anne Spendiff   109
10 Emancipating Rita: the limits of change
     Sue Gollop   130

References   144
Index   150

Series editor's introduction

Over the years there has been much written for and about teachers and teaching. However, little can be heard within this vast and various literature of the voices of teachers themselves. Why do books about teachers' thinking and practice tend not to be written by teachers themselves? There are many reasons for this, involving history and tradition as well as opportunity; and there are some who would add power and control (by one group over another). Whatever the reasons, it is a matter of concern that research into the practice of those who work in schools and other organizations should be documented and made public. Colin Biott and Jennifer Nias, the editors of this collection, have worked over many years with and alongside teachers, encouraging and challenging them in processes of individual and collaborative reflection on their practice and supporting them in the often painful, lengthy process of perspective transformation which may result. It is not surprising, then, that these two practitioners should bring together a collection of writings that represent and express their own ideals and values of, for example, the power of talk in helping to bring about change, the importance of not divorcing the study of practical activity from the study of thinking, and the recognition that quality growth occurs over time through collaboration rather than 'quick fix' events which reinforce professional isolation.

The chapters in this book are written in a variety of styles, from professional critique to narrative, personal testimony and even polemic. All, however, provide authoritative evidence that teachers and others who undertake academically demanding courses *do* benefit in terms of professional as well as personal development, and that this does have direct benefits to their places of work; and all provide evidence of the powerful emancipating effect of the use of systematic reflection upon one's thinking and practice. The book contains chapters on pre-service, in-service and adult education generally, and a particularly thought provoking section on learning and change from a feminist perspective. It will be useful to all who wish to learn more about effective ways of developing their own and others' reflective practice and of managing change; and it will be of particular interest because it is written principally from a practitioner perspective.

Christopher Day

Notes on contributors

Kate Ashcroft is a tutor at Westminster College, Oxford. She is responsible for all aspects of the DipHE and BEd courses and has undertaken research into enquiry-based initial teacher education courses.

Sheena Ball is headteacher of Melin Junior School, Neath, West Glamorgan. She is concerned to self-evaluate her practice and encourage staff development.

Colin Biott is Reader in Education Studies at Newcastle upon Tyne Polytechnic. He is leader of the enquiry-based MEd course and is involved in research and evaluation projects in a number of LEAs.

Penelope Campbell is an advisory teacher for primary education in Essex. She has participated in research on whole school curriculum development in primary schools.

Andy Convery teaches at Cleveland College. He is currently working with a colleague to examine how teachers' personal interests influence classroom processes.

Sue Gollop was Principal Lecturer in Primary Education at Hatfield Polytechnic when she undertook her research with mature students. She is now a primary adviser with Hertfordshire LEA.

Mary Heath is deputy head (and full-time class teacher) at Rice Trevor Lower School, Bromham, Bedfordshire.

Jay Mawdsley was Coordinator of the National Writing Project, Newcastle upon Tyne. She is currently working with a wide range of schools in her position of general adviser (English).

Jennifer Nias is a tutor at the Cambridge Institute of Education. She works with teachers on a variety of in-service courses and has directed and participated in research into staff relationships in primary schools.

Anne Spendiff is a women's education tutor in the north-east of England. She is also a mother and is active in the women's movement.

Robin Yeomans is Senior Lecturer in Primary Education at Bedford College of Higher Education. There he works on both pre-service and in-service courses for teachers and has a particular research interest in primary school staff relationships and in groups in general.

Acknowledgements

The editors are grateful to Basil Blackwell for permission to use the extract from A. Clegg (1980) *About Our Schools*, which appears in Chapter 5.

We are also very appreciative of the unfailing and patient support we have received from the staff of the Cambridge Institute of Education and New-castle Polytechnic Department of Education Studies.

Introduction

Jennifer Nias

Working and learning together may easily become conservative activities. By contrast, and by definition, working or learning together for change have developmental purposes. This is a book about partnerships entered into and sustained with a view to making some change in the educational process or systems. It is built upon personal accounts, each of which addresses from a different perspective the book's central theme and makes a particular contribution to our understanding of its possibilities and complexities.

The contributors have drawn upon their experience of a wide range of collaborative relationships. Teachers describe working in partnership with their students. There are many examples of peers, be they teachers or students, working and learning together, and of senior and junior colleagues in schools and colleges developing productive partnerships. Some people (for example, advisory teachers, teachers with staff development responsibilities, college of education tutors, headteachers) see themselves as having a formal responsibility to help others change; others have taken on the role incidentally, as part of or a corollary to other posts. Generally, collaboration took place only in the workplace, although sometimes (e.g. Chapter 6) a group met outside school to extend the partnerships established within it and, more rarely, groups were established outside schools. Several of the accounts analyse the experience of people working together across institutional boundaries (e.g. teachers visiting colleges of education; tutors and students on teaching practice; advisory teachers; advisers). Other groups and partnerships flourished within a single school or college. Sometimes individuals participated, whether as teachers or students, in several partnerships that either existed simultaneously or overlapped in time or space.

It was also possible for different opportunities to work collaboratively to occur sequentially.

Reflecting this richness and diversity, we have divided the chapters into three parts which should be regarded as overlapping and interconnected. The tripartite arrangement is for the convenience of the reader and should not be taken as suggesting that the topic 'working and learning together for change' can be tidily or easily dissected into discrete themes. Indeed, the purpose of this introduction is to draw attention to ideas and issues which occur in several or all of the chapters and which appear to be central to an understanding of collaborative development at any level and in all parts of the educational system.

The first part of the book presents the ideas and analyses the experience of those who cross institutional boundaries in order to help others change. It focuses upon the work of advisory and support teachers and upon developments in initial teacher education which specifically seek to promote in student teachers an understanding that teachers have to work with adults as well as with children, and that they therefore need to develop appropriate understandings, attitudes and interpersonal skills.

The second part presents the personal experiences of a middle school deputy, a primary school head, a teacher in a further education college and two coordinators of the National Writing Project. They all set out to work with others in order to bring about change but found that their own learning was enhanced in the process. Their foci are the subjective realities of collaboration and of change.

The third part critically addresses the claims, implicitly or explicitly made by many feminists, that women are particularly well equipped to work in collaboration with one another, that their shared activities have the potential for mutual consciousness-raising and that this experience itself involves a type of learning so profound that it may be described as emancipatory. Both the contributors to this section write as teachers of adults, and reflect upon their own learning and development as they worked to facilitate change in their students.

A major theme which runs through many of the chapters is the purposes for which adults work or learn together in schools and colleges. So closely related to this that it cannot be separated from it is a sub-theme: the variety of forms taken by such collaboration. In the past two decades much attention has quite properly focused upon the interactions that take place between teachers and students, especially in classrooms. Less emphasis has been placed upon the reasons why and the ways in which staff members work together, and upon tutors' and students' experiences of collaborative teaching methods in colleges and other adult education settings. Yet our contributors make it clear that adults are productively working and learning together in all parts of the educational system. The time therefore seems ripe for a further collaborative act: the publication under joint editorship of a number of analytic accounts of the professional experiences of those who are extending our knowledge in this field.

The book also seeks to show how difficult it is in educational settings to make or sustain the distinction between 'working' and 'learning'. Teachers who set up and participate in collaborative activities usually do so for professional reasons, that is to enhance peers' or students' learning, whether directly or indirectly. Working together in schools and colleges has an educative intent. Similarly, learning together takes place within a work-oriented context. Sometimes people, be they students or teachers, are asked to collaborate on a task in the expectation that they will thereby learn how to work together; at other times they learn from one another as a by-product of tackling a problem or an activity of joint concern. Whether tasks requiring collaboration are set up with explicit learning goals in mind or result in unanticipated learning, they are educational in outcome. Moreover, even when collaboration (e.g. between teachers or between teachers and their students) takes place in order to enhance students' learning, teachers themselves often also develop and change in the process. The accounts in this book show them learning from their students and their peers – about themselves, about learning and teaching, about the process of critical enquiry – and illustrate how learners may teach one another. In other words, in the experience of these authors the processes of 'working' and 'learning' have the potential continually to flow into and enrich each other. Shared responsibility for learning may become a cooperative task which in turn leads to the development among participants of fresh insights, new skills or altered perspectives. Similarly, working together on an activity not directly related to learning can stimulate and nourish growth, while learning together may develop a sense of mutual responsibility for the accomplishment of agreed goals and so lead in the future to further collaboration. Indeed, Nias *et al.* (1992) found that the mutually supportive relationship which existed between working and learning together was a central aspect of successful whole-school curriculum development in the primary schools they studied. Of course, not all educational encounters or establishments have the vigorous, yeasty quality of these schools; educational settings can be as socially and professionally sterile as any other. However, we hope that the chapters in this book suggest the natural affinity that many people at all levels of the educational system now find to exist between cooperation on tasks and professional development.

In this context, it is relevant that many of our contributors began the work about which they write as part of their own professional learning. With the exception of Colin Biott, Robin Yeomans and Kate Ashcroft, all the authors have been recent students on extended courses that have required them to look analytically and rigorously at their own practice and to share the process of critical enquiry with fellow course members and with colleagues in their schools and colleges. The remaining authors and the two editors are tutors to such courses. Those who have written this book have themselves found that it is hard to distinguish between working and learning. As they have taught, and reflected critically upon their practice in order to fulfil the requirements of their courses, they have increased their professional knowledge and skills and changed their assumptions and attitudes. This fact has an important bearing upon the claim, sometimes made by those outside the profession, that teachers who undertake academically demanding courses benefit in terms of personal rather than professional development. It is obvious from the studies presented here that this is not the case: the educational work of these teachers and their colleagues has benefited from the learning demands of the courses they have undertaken, and their learning has been enhanced by its practical focus and nature. To be sure, several write of the personal growth that has resulted from their involvement in the processes of critical enquiry and collaborative reflection, but they see this increased self-knowledge and insight as having professional relevance because it has enhanced their understanding of their work and their capacity to undertake it effectively.

The chapters carry a further common message. They all emphasize the value of systematic and critical self-study as the basis for productive professional development. Some writers (e.g. Kate Ashcroft, Sheena Ball, Andy Convery) emphasize the value to themselves and others of embarking upon an action research cycle, both as a means of focusing individuals' attention upon issues that are of practical significance to them and as a way of promoting thoughtful action. Others (e.g. Robin Yeomans, Jay Mawdsley, Mary Heath) stress the importance of a stable group of colleagues who share in the interpretation of evidence, in the processes of analysis and questioning which throw new light upon the familiar, and in the search for practicable solutions to individual problems. Sue Gollop and Anne Spendiff set both action research and collaborative enquiry within the wider intellectual frameworks of critical and feminist theory. Colin Biott brings many of these strands together in a typology which contrasts a 'developmental' and an 'implementation' model of advisory teachers' work. Together these accounts and analyses provide a powerful critique of forms of professional development activity which adopt a wholly didactic pedagogy, look for swift results at technical levels of classroom action and behaviour, implicitly divorce practical activity from thinking, and encourage professional isolation and individualism. Rather, this book proposes, and provides evidence of, an approach to professional development which enables individuals, working with supportive but challenging peers and teacher-facilitators, critically to examine their assumptions, thought processes and actions and to try out and examine alternatives. The professional change that results grows from reflective examination of the self, not from the exhortations of others; from evidence not from assertion; from the thoughtful examination of multiple rather than single perspectives; from small steps taken with support not great strides attempted in isolation. However, as these accounts also suggest, professional change is neither swiftly nor easily accomplished, even when it arises out of and is supported by collaborative activity. Each chapter in some way throws light on the nature and felt experience of radical change, whether in thinking or behaviour. They all stress that it is a difficult and painful process; Sue Gollop shows that it may not happen at all.

The glacial slowness of change in education is now almost a truism. Recent explanations (e.g. Fullan 1991; Nias *et al.* 1992) for teachers' reluctance to alter their pedagogical behaviour have stressed the fact that individuals' beliefs and values are at the heart of their behaviour and that it is hard to effect change at this level of the human personality. Furthermore, Pollard (1985), Nias (1989) and Woods (1991) have all stressed the importance to teachers of maintaining, in and out of the classroom, their own sense of identity, of the sort of people and practitioners that they perceive themselves to be. In addition, Nias and Woods have argued that at the heart of this self-image is a well-defended core of self-defining attitudes and values. If teachers want to adopt new forms of classroom organization or curriculum materials, adapt to different administrative structures, or change superficial aspects of their teaching behaviour, they appear to be able to do so fairly easily. By contrast, they find it extremely difficult to alter their educational, social or moral beliefs and values or the 'practical theories' (Elliott 1976) which underpin their minute-by-minute actions and decisions. As a result they also find it very hard to modify the behaviours which most closely reflect the sense of personal identity in which these beliefs and theories are embedded. Put another way, they find it much easier to alter the technical means by which they seek to fulfil their aims than to examine or modify the aims themselves. To recognize and change one's 'basic assumptions' (Abercrombie 1969) calls for a shift in professional self-perception so radical that it has been described as 'perspective transformation' (Mezirow 1981). Colin Biott further explores this idea in his chapter. Such a change, as Anne Spendiff and Sue Gollop show, is also at the heart of the consciousness-raising that plays an important part in the thinking of feminists and critical theorists.

Change at the level of beliefs and assumptions is not only difficult to achieve, it is also slow and, since it is usually attended by conflict and guilt, it is often accompanied by suffering. Indeed Nias (1991) likens change in an individual's core of self-defining beliefs to bereavement, a loss so profound that it calls for the gradual construction of a new identity upon, but wherever possible within, the ruins of the old. These too are themes which recur throughout this book. Each account stresses the slowness of any change that affects teachers' or student teachers' beliefs and values and that thereby challenges their sense of self. Many emphasize the painful nature of the self-realization upon which the change process depends and of the transition from one form of self-definition to another. Several refer to the individual's feelings of anxiety and self-doubt during the lengthy process of self-discovery and self-conscious modification. Many tell of teachers and students who have critically explored their practice, and examined themselves in relation to others, but who have also, in the process, experienced a sense of vulnerability and encountered fear.

Andy Convery and Jay Mawdsley suggest that one of the main sources of fear for teachers is that of losing control. Teachers, we suggest, are particularly vulnerable because of the occupational importance which is attached to 'being in control'. They do not feel that they have attained a full professional identity until they are 'in control', customarily they believe that they are judged (by pupils, parents, superiors, peers) in terms of their ability to maintain discipline over children, and many fear their own capacity for violent or unruly behaviour when provoked or under stress (Nias 1989). The sense of powerlessness which attends any change in self-image is thus aggravated for teachers by the fear that their ability as practitioners is being called into question. This is particularly the case when, as has been the case for many educationalists following the Education Act of 1988, such change is imposed from outside.

The fact that teachers are socialized into a personal respect and occupational need for control tends also to encourage them to be authority-dependent. Sheena Ball and Penelope Campbell take up this theme, pointing out the problems which beset headteachers and other senior managers who attempt to involve others for the first time in collaborative decision-making. One effect of a hierarchical system of staff management is that participants do not initially wish to accept formal control over their own affairs when it is offered to them. Andy Convery, Sue Gollop and Robin Yeomans suggest that this is also true of the management of teaching and that students may initially reject their teachers' open or tacit invitation to them to become autonomous learners. The situation is further complicated, as Colin Biott and Andy Convery stress, by the fact that teachers do not readily surrender control over the curriculum, teaching methods, management or organization of their classrooms. Nias *et al.* (1992) suggest that the answer to this apparent inconsistency lies in teachers' sense of moral responsibility for their students and for the latter's learning and, consequently, in their felt need to exercise control over every aspect of the learning situation for which they perceive themselves to be responsible. Since, however, they often expect their formal leaders to be responsible for the wider aspects of their students' education (e.g. discipline outside the classroom, curriculum policies, resource provision), they feel that the latter should be in control of these. The reluctance of many teachers to share in the governance and administration of schools and colleges stems from the close relationship which appears to exist between responsibility and the right to control. Indeed, all the chapters in one way or another address the problem that, whereas the development of collaborative relationships involves a willingness to share with others both responsibility for a working or learning situation and control over it, teachers are not traditionally used to sharing with others either of these aspects of their professional practice.

Although this book stresses the hard, slow and painful nature of fundamental change in education, it also explicates and illustrates the roles that others may play in helping to bring about and sustain such change. It stresses in particular the value of: support and reinforcement; enquiry and cognitive challenge; creating a common language for discussion; modelling alternative forms of behaviour.

Whether teachers and learners are working or learning together, their interaction in pursuit of common goals puts them in a good position to support one another across the frightening chasm of personal and professional change. Robin Yeomans, Kate Ashcroft, Sheena Ball, Jay Mawdsley and Colin Biott draw attention to the fact that if such interactions are to become possible, adults must learn appropriate interpersonal attitudes and skills. A willingness to give and take help within a context of mutual respect does not come naturally to many participants in an educational system which traditionally emphasizes individualism, authority-dependence and, frequently, competition; nor, similarly, does the ability to support, encourage and listen to others. Kate Ashcroft and Robin Yeomans in particular argue that the education of teachers should include structured experience in work-oriented groups and the opportunity to reflect with others upon the processes of collaboration. Mary Heath, Anne Spendiff and Sue Gollop suggest that members of women's groups are especially skilled in giving one another the kind of support which helps to raise collective and individual consciousness of alternative perspectives and actions and which encourages individuals while they work out for themselves new identities and ways of behaving. Such groups are particularly supportive because they tend to be egalitarian rather than hierarchical in structure, with leadership moving between members in response to the task and to individual capabilities, because individuals' personal concerns are regarded as a legitimate part of the group's agenda and because emotion is perceived as a natural part of members' reactions to and interactions with one another. Anne Spendiff makes it clear that to hold a role as formal leader within such a group, for instance as tutor, can in itself be difficult, because the responsibility and control which are traditionally associated with such a position conflict with the egalitarian nature and structure of women's interactions with one another. Robin Yeomans also feels that active membership of staff groups in primary schools calls for a 'flat' and shifting leadership structure, for acceptance of members as people as well as professionals and therefore for the expression of feelings as a natural part of working and learning together. In other words, he sees as characteristic of 'collaborative school cultures' (Nias *et al.* 1989) styles of interacting which others perceive as feminist. Of course, many primary schools are predominantly staffed by women and it may be that a particular type of school culture has evolved as a result, without being identified or perceived as gender-determined. Without further evidence it is difficult to resolve this question. One may, however, speculate that an increase in cooperative working in educational institutions and the marked growth of staff gender ratios dominated by women may lead in the future to the evolution of a new 'matriarchal' style of leadership in education which differs in several important respects from the patriarchal and, some would suggest, Judaeo-Hebraic (and Islamic) forms to which we are accustomed.

Members of partnerships and collaborative groups do not simply offer one another affective support as together they face change. All the accounts in this book also suggest that as they work or learn together individuals effect cognitive changes in one another. The themes of enquiry and challenge feature in every chapter. All the accounts suggest, though in different contexts and with reference to a variety of partnerships, that teachers can help one another to change and to adapt to new situations: by offering each other fresh ways of looking at familiar situations, by interpreting evidence in different ways, by airing disagreements or differences of opinion and by sharing aspects of their own experience which conflict with those of others – in short, by opening the way for, and sustaining the impetus towards, the 'perspective transformation' (Mezirow 1981) or 'new comprehension' (Wilson *et al.* 1987) which Colin Biott argues is a necessary corollary to a developmental partnership.

There is some suggestion in these chapters that challenge is a particularly important ingredient in productive relationships between school leaders. Yet, although it is clear from the chapters in sections 2 and 3 that collaboration is possible only when there is some agreement among any participants on ends, or a willingness, as Colin Biott suggests, to engage in enquiry so as to discover a shared goal, these accounts also make it plain that agreement does not have to be total or absolute. Sheena Ball stresses how valuable, though painful, she found it to have a deputy with a tireless appetite for informed argument. Penelope Campbell's story describes a more subtle form of dialectic. She suggests that there was some felt agreement between one head and deputy at the level of values. This 'accord' enabled them temporarily to put aside their differences in relation to other educational aims and to embark on making and implementing a school development plan. As they worked together to engage the staff in this process, they influenced and learnt from one another. A shared sense that they could 'get along together' engendered sufficient mutual trust to enable debate about means. The challenge that they thereby offered to one another simultaneously changed them both and opened up the possibility of constructive disagreement on other ends.

This and other chapters suggest that the most productive challenges offered by others are often small and incremental rather than wide-ranging and fundamental. This relates to two occupational characteristics of the teaching profession to which we have already drawn attention: the centrality to teachers' purposes of their self-defining values and their felt need to control themselves and their environment. When cognitive challenge is offered within a fruitful partnership (such as that of the heads and deputies described by Sheena Ball and Penelope Campbell or the tutor–student relationship of which Sue Gollop writes) it means that both partners are working to define their purposes jointly and to share control over them. Yet giving up control over ends involves the risk that change may move in directions with which one is not in sympathy. As Sheena Ball points out, she was not able to begin to enable change among her staff until she allowed them to determine the direction of this for themselves, a form of behaviour which required that, as a head, she first let go of her desire to control their teaching. Colin Biott, Sue Gollop, Andy Convery and Robin Yeomans tell similar stories, all of which suggest that becoming an effective partner or group member involves surrendering the right to determine by oneself the direction or nature of change. Small wonder that when members of the educational system are working or learning together, they find it easier and more productive to move slowly towards fundamental changes through a series of jointly and pragmatically determined shifts than they do to try to determine in advance fixed, long-term aims.

Running through every contributor's experience of both support and challenge are references to the power of talk in helping to bring about change. Every chapter mentions discussion between participants. Most emphasize its centrality, as a means of reflecting on common or vicarious experience, exchanging information and opinions, raising fresh ideas or possibilities and, in the process, of negotiating shared meanings for the words through which conversation itself takes place. Mary Heath in particular stresses the latter aspect of shared talk, arguing that members of her National Writing Project group came only slowly to understand one another's meanings and that their capacity to work and learn together was greatly enhanced by the development of the common understandings which gradually grew from their frequent discussions.

Actions were also important. Sometimes, as Colin Biott, Sheena Ball and Penelope Campbell suggest, they served as a sign to participants of the existence of shared values or aims (or in one case cited by Robin Yeomans of a mismatch between a new head and the existing staff culture). At others, they enabled one person or group to facilitate change in others by providing a powerful example, or model, both of what was possible and of how it might be achieved. Colin Biott, Robin Yeomans, Penelope Campbell, Sheena Ball and Andy Convery all stress, with reference to different educational settings, that deeds can sometimes be more persuasive than words and that more credence is attached in schools and colleges to what people do than to what they say.

One final point remains to be made. It concerns the organizational contexts in which our contributors 'worked and learned together for change'. As Andy Convery and Sheena Ball show, collaboration and the professional development which it engenders are seriously retarded when institutional structures and procedures deprive participants of time and opportunities to meet. Pressures also come from outside the school or college, especially as a result of recent legislative changes, such as the introduction of the National Curriculum and of the local management of schools. Colin Biott, Jay Mawdsley and Mary Heath in particular stress that teachers perceive their teaching commitments as their prime responsibility. They now face so many other additional and competing demands upon their time that it is often difficult for them to sustain collaborative relationships.

This, then, is a book written by practitioners who have worked and learned with others and who have attempted to distil from that experience the reasons for and means by which it has contributed to change – within themselves, within others, within their own organizations and within other parts of the educational system. Although the experience of each contributor is unique, the stories which they tell and their analytic commentaries upon these have much in common. The parts into which the book is divided indicate only one of the many ways in which the issues that they address can be grouped together. Running through and across the various chapters are other unifying themes. These relate to the nature and purposes of collaboration among adults in the educational system; to the efficacy of systematic, reflective self-study and critical enquiry, especially when under-taken with others; to the difficulty and felt experience of educational change and to the ways in which others may contribute to initiating, sustaining or impeding it. The book itself is the product of many different but fruitful partnerships; our hope is that it may encourage others along a similar road, towards their own forms of shared professional development.

Part I

Working together to help others change

Imposed support for teachers' learning: implementation or development partnerships?

Colin Biott

In the past few years many of us have been offered support by people whose jobs have been to help us to improve our work in line with mandated change. At best there has been a well-intentioned attempt to seek our commitment and then, ironically, to give us what is called 'ownership' of the new skills and attitudes. At worst the problems have been thrust upon us at an inconvenient time, often with little or no choice about whether we wished to be advised or supported. The feeling induced is reminiscent of that of a colleague who sidled up to me during an end of term social gathering, looked at his watch, and asked quietly, 'How long do you think that we are expected to stay here enjoying ourselves like this?'

In order to develop a critique of obligatory, 'official' support for change, this chapter will focus on the job of advisory teaching. When they give up the relative security of their own classrooms to help other teachers, advisory teachers soon gain experience of the intricacies of 'working and learning together for change'. To paraphrase the title of this book, they are an example of professional 'workers-and-learners-together-for-change'. To spend their time working with other teachers is their central task, and not just an enhancement of it.

Sullivan (1991), for instance, is generally positive about his experience of advisory teaching, but he also catches the awkwardness of imposed support when he says:

> There was frequently a sense of unease by the classteachers as to why they had been singled out for 'support'. Was it because their teaching was regarded as inadequate, or because they were a 'soft target' on the staff.
>
> (Sullivan 1991: 47)

This chapter signals caution about the assumption that advisory teaching will inevitably lead to long-term change. This is not to question the competence, diligence or motivation of individuals. The problems arise partly from the contrived circumstances in which the work is attempted and partly from lack of clarity about the relationship between the approaches used and the kind of professional learning which is intended. The ideas in this chapter derive from five separate studies of advisory teacher projects in three separate local education authorities (LEAs), including an evaluation of a whole support service. References are also made to recent literature on teacher leadership, and professional and school development in North America and the UK.

I have written elsewhere about how it feels to do such a demanding and difficult job (Biott 1991). In this chapter I shall first explore some features of the imposed, and therefore often uncomfortable and impracticable, situations in which advisory teachers may find themselves working. Some of the problems remain hidden because, like most teachers, advisory teachers are inclined to find ways to make the best of inconvenience and to make the unmanageable appear possible. The second section is focused upon the ways in which they work with teachers and on the kinds of learning that their work might support.

Overall, the chapter will emphasize that it is important to avoid standardized policies of implementation, to take account of the varied contexts in which support is offered and to be realistic about the kind of learning that a particular approach may yield. If such a potentially rich resource remains available during a period of financial constraint, both headteachers and project coordinators should ensure that advisory teachers' time is spent profitably. The chapter ends by proposing principles for a development model rather than an implementation model of support for teachers' learning.

Working together in enforced circumstances: problems of imposition

There is evidence that advisory teachers are highly regarded, credible and popular. A recent HMI report (DES 1989b) outlines their function broadly as 'to work alongside other teachers in respect of the development of a subject or an aspect of the curriculum and to be responsible to the adviser/ inspector for that area of the curriculum' (paragraph 3.14), and describes them as 'highly motivated, hard working and, in some cases, inspirational in their teaching and support of schools'. Nevertheless, it is sensible to be cautious about what some 'official' attempts to get teachers to work and learn together for change might achieve. The following ideas are not intended to be exhaustive, but they illustrate some of the instances when problems arise because of the enforced circumstances in which the work is attempted.

When the host teachers 'resist meddling'

Rather than blaming teachers for resisting imposed and unwelcome innovations, Wolcott (1977) has recognized his own tendency as an anthropologist to side with the underdog. He has tried to understand how teachers 'resist the meddling' of those who attempt to change them. One way for them to do this is to appear to accept the innovation rather than to take a stand against it. He saw that it was then possible for the teachers to carry on doing what they had been doing with some relatively inconsequential tokens of compliance.

In the same way, rather than draw attention to themselves through direct refusal or protest, it is generally prudent for busy teachers to agree to work with advisory teachers and then to engage in temporary and undemanding work which will yield little or no lasting change. However sceptical a teacher might be, it is sometimes sensible to accept resources, to tolerate being told and even to suffer being shown what to do. At the same time it is unlikely that the advisory teachers will want to be a cause of vexation, worry or embarrassment so they will probably have tactics for being seen as necessarily busy, but helpfully unthreatening. This results in an unspoken truce in which they work together without intending to learn together.

When the advisory teachers play safe to avoid meddling

During an evaluation study of an Educational Support Grant Project in targeted urban primary schools, the advisory teachers recalled how they were aware of the need to be undemanding and to offer immediate, practical assistance to teachers: to be a second pair of hands. The 'official' aims of the project, to improve both the host teachers' expectations and the curriculum of the schools, provided a background against which it was wise to try to build relationships with sensitivity and patience. As a teacher in another school told them, 'You're like a red rag to a bull in there.' In the early stages, they found themselves engaged in a series of fragmented activities, such as making resources, arranging and helping with children's visits out of school without any involvement in follow-up work, working with groups outside of the classrooms, being limited to small, specific tasks in the confines of a corner of the room, and even 'covering' for teachers who were then able to leave their classrooms and go elsewhere.

Similar problems which I have identified, through recent studies of advisory and support teachers' work, include:

1 Times when the desire for a reputation as a hard worker and consequent attempts to work with a lot of teachers means that the advisory teachers spread themselves too thinly to achieve working partnerships of sufficient depth to promote teacher development.

2 Occasions when the fear of rejection by teachers weakens advisory teachers' resolve and dilutes both their work and the criteria for judging its
  progress. This also leads, in extreme cases, to a sense of being manipulated.
3 Those times when the wish to establish credibility as a teacher with
  special skills increases the temptation to perform familiar, set-piece, dem-
  onstration lessons. The responsiveness and liveliness of primary school
  children can make this especially seductive for ex-secondary school
  teachers.

Underlying these problems is the advisory teacher's uneasy feeling of
being of only marginal use to the teachers. Little (1988) has argued, from
her analysis of the California Mentor Teacher Program, that the day-to-day
organization of schools is in any case not usually conducive to teacher
leadership:

> Teachers placed in positions that bear the titles and resources of
> leadership display a caution towards their colleagues that is both
> poignant and eminently sensible. The relation with other teachers that
> is implied by terms like mentor, advisor or specialist has little place in
> the ordinary workings of most schools. Even the simple etiquette of
> teacher leadership is unclear.
>
>   (Little 1988: 84)

She has observed how teacher leaders in the USA have almost rendered
themselves useless through zealously playing down their 'expertness'. She
cites two key factors which reduce the prospects for teacher leadership: the
unwillingness of most teachers to accept the idea of the 'master teacher'
(sic) who could advise them, and the scarcity of school cultures in which
teachers can gain a close working knowledge of each other's work, based
upon observation and in-depth discussion.

A further factor which can blunt the challenge of support for teachers'
learning is the tendency of those managing advisory teachers to pay attention
to what McNeil (1988) has called 'smooth running'. She says that schools
can sometimes displace their main goal of encouraging quality learning by
the ritual of seeming to do so. What becomes most important is that things
run smoothly.

In the case of advisory teaching, the emphasis on 'smooth running' can
lead to an over-concentration on the interpersonal dimension so that the
achievement of harmony outweighs analysis and challenge. There is also a
tendency for the coordinator of a support service, especially during periods
of vulnerability about its public image, to bend over backwards to avoid
friction with the schools, and to introduce standard policies and procedures
which lean towards playing safe. Where this occurs, the emphasis is on
service rather than learning, on sameness rather than diversity and on fairness
instead of suitability to context.

In circumstances where the prospects for genuine learning partnerships are weak, it is likely that the contribution of external advisory teachers will be blunted. There might be plenty of effort and activity, but little depth and continuity and no direction.

When host teachers and advisory teachers make 'symbolic agreements'

The least demanding kind of working together is coordinated planning at a distance from the classroom. Even so, the results will not always be useful. When the purpose for planning is imposed, when there is lack of time and when there are divergent interests and priorities, the result will probably be little more than a set of 'symbolic agreements' (Bredo and Bredo 1975). 'Symbolic agreements' are most often found where there are

> potentially divergent interests, with tenuous bonds between partici-
> pants loosely allied in a common endeavour, and where time for
> reaching agreement is limited. Under such conditions, specific details
> are avoided and potential differences are smoothed over in hope that
> common ideals will draw participants to a common allegiance. Such
> agreements are vague enough to allow latitude for each participant to
> imagine that his preferences are represented.
>
> (Bredo and Bredo 1975: 462)

The concept of the 'symbolic agreement' is useful for understanding how circumstances can weaken the impact of much of the planning that takes place between advisory and host teachers when they make arrangements to work together. Much of the planning is attempted by comparative strangers in snatched moments between lessons. Furthermore, both partners are often aware that they are only agreeing to something brief and transitory. In one large LEA, for example, the advisory teachers for primary science and technology were attempting to share their time equally between all the schools over a three-year period. This meant that each school received about five days support, to be divided among all its teachers. A survey of 340 of the participating teachers revealed that most of them (69 per cent) had only had brief informal chats to plan and review their work with the advisory teachers.

As one advisory teacher commented: 'We try to have ten minutes or so to evaluate at the end of a lesson, but there is pressure of time on class teachers, and for me too, to prepare for the next session. It tends to be often done while we clear away.' This observation is not made in order to attach blame to teachers. Sullivan (1991) has caught the awkwardness of their position when he says that he was:

very conscious of the relentless conflicting pressures and demands on teachers' attention and time. Discussion seemed invariably to focus on practical problems and short-term objectives rather than exploring long-term goals and the theory underlying the work.

(Sullivan 1991: 47)

Mere symbolic agreements are made when there is no attempt to reconcile the differences between aims and when potential disagreements are masked or deferred. Subsequently, the partners engage in parallel working, which is often not sustained long enough for differences to become apparent.

When the imposed support arrangements ignore teachers' work patterns

Teachers, like other occupational groups, find ways to adapt to their working environment, not only to manage their own participation in the classroom, but also to pace themselves throughout the whole working day. When, for instance, do they do their preparation, marking and administration? What happens in formal and informal meetings between colleagues, and what is the effect of the time and place of the meetings? How do they balance periods of intense effort with the need for relaxation and recuperation? Which non-teaching tasks are imposed on teachers and which are self-initiated, which tasks must be undertaken at a specified time and which can be accomplished whenever the teacher chooses, even outside of the 'official working day'? How does the inclusion of an obligation, such as a formal staff meeting during lunch-time, or a yard-duty, or a self-appointed task like running a chess club, affect the teachers' working rhythms and feelings about other activities during that day?

Questions like these are important when we come to think about the ways that teachers might be expected to work and learn together. In a recent study (Biott *et al.* 1989) 55 primary school teachers were interviewed about their views of professional development. Their responses showed that they had valued spontaneous and informal learning from colleagues during their careers, and also highlighted the importance of the dynamics of their own working patterns and relationships.

When asked to describe, without naming them, the current colleagues from whom they learnt during the working day they referred to the following personal qualities and professional attitudes and skills:

- is approachable, has vision, is enthusiastic and inspiring, works hard, seeks to improve;
- experiments, has ideas, willingly discusses ideas, doesn't care about making mistakes, learns from mistakes;
- motivates children, achieves high standards, has caring relationships with children;

- has all round primary competence, good classroom organization, lots of ideas and approaches in all curriculum areas.

As well as being valued for their contributions to designated training events, colleagues with these qualities were also sources of informal and spontaneous learning through 'popping into classrooms' and casual conversations. The teachers thought that opportunities for exchanging ideas had increased recently:

> We've looked at things more closely in the last two years as we are all in the same boat.

> The national curriculum has influenced us. We've had to work together as a school.

Less positively, factors which inhibited or limited learning often arose from the ways in which formal leadership was allocated. In some cases it had:

- added pressure to staff who were given inappropriate leadership positions;
- prevented some teachers' talents from being tapped or caused them to 'hold back' from giving support because this was somebody else's job;
- prevented some teachers from giving support to others because their subject area was not the current priority and so they had little 'air-time'.

When talking about formal courses in their LEA the teachers also mentioned occasional problems arising from imposed participation. Many reported being with fellow participants who had been 'sent' to courses and who were sometimes directly negative or took the opportunity to display general cynicism. This soured the atmosphere and restricted the learning of the more committed.

Hargreaves (1990) has developed a micro-political critique of collegiality among teachers in which he has pointed to the differences between administratively imposed and controlled forms of collegiality, and the more evolutionary and spontaneous forms which are sustained by the teachers themselves. The former he calls 'contrived collegiality', when 'administrators insist that teachers meet together (in scheduled time) and for the purposes that administrators determine' (Hargreaves 1990: 17). He makes the following distinctions between 'contrived collegiality' and 'collaborative cultures':

Contrived collegiality	*Collaborative cultures*
Administratively regulated	Spontaneous
Compulsory	Voluntary
Implementation-oriented	Development-oriented
Fixed in time and place	Pervasive in time and space
Predictable	Unpredictable

He further argues that under conditions of contrived collegiality teachers are not being empowered but are being required or persuaded to work together to implement the mandates of others. His study in Canadian schools showed, for example, that when some schools have scheduled periods of preparation time as a way of facilitating collaborative planning they are not always used for this purpose. Some teachers

> would retreat to their own room or other space, to work alone, for their own classes, clearing away the plethora of little tasks for which preparation time is seen as so important. Yet in doing so, they would feel guilty, aware that they were going against the wishes of their principal.
>
> (Hargreaves 1990: 22)

Teachers' use of time could not be standardized through imposed routines. It was clearly adaptive to daily and weekly variations in circumstances and priorities. Flexibility and the teachers' own judgements and discretion were the key elements.

When there are problems about expertise and control in partnerships

Hargreaves (1990) suggests that two other factors compounded the complexity of imposed working partnerships: those of 'expertise' and 'control'. These factors were apparent when some teachers were given time to plan their work with special education resource teachers. What was important was whether or not the host teacher would acknowledge the complementary expertise of the resource teacher. Where the class teachers thought that they know as much as the resource teachers, the scheduled meetings were thought to be redundant. In these cases, they met infrequently.

The issue of control became significant when the role of the resource teacher was widened from withdrawing pupils from the classroom to having a whole-class function alongside the teacher. There were some clashes, for instance, about who should deal with mainstream pupils in the classroom. Overall, the difficulties caused by this kind of 'contrived collegiality' arose from the class teachers' desire to maintain control, without experiencing interference. Nias et al. (1991) also found this urge to control but they have linked it with the teachers' sense of accountability and responsibility rather than with insecurity or 'bossiness'.

Gillman (1990) also saw control as an inportant dimension in his study of an internal support teaching programme in a comprehensive school. The teachers' own styles and particularly their attitudes to classroom control were key factors. A partnership was only likely to flourish if there was an intuitive sense of compatibility regardless of the formal policy statement and prescribed code of conduct. The working relationships were often achieved informally by 'fitting in' and 'feeling the ground'.

> You might feel that you are trespassing on someone's sort of . . . you know ground. Like discipline particularly. Because people have different ways of disciplining – I mean some people have ways of disciplining in a very quiet sort of way. At first you think they're not doing very much but they have a very tight control on the kids. You sort of have to look for it. Other people are sort of noisy and voluble and all the rest of it, so you have to sort of fit in with the person. You've got to feel the ground out for a while and fit in with them.
>
> (Support teacher in interview)

Many teachers and advisory teachers will recognize some of the problems raised in this part of the chapter. Such difficulties often arise when standardized policies and imposed strategies of support are applied without regard for the spontaneous, informal working patterns of those involved. Because of the different conditions in which work is attempted it is prudent to avoid over-ambitious, generalized claims about teachers working and learning together for change. Hargreaves's comparison of 'development' and 'implementation' oriented working relationships raises an important distinction which I shall explore in the next part of the chapter. For the purposes of the discussion it may be helpful to describe extreme forms of implementation and development partnerships between advisory teachers and class teachers. Implementation is characterized by an emphasis on the achievement of short-term, predictable goals and on discharging defined duties in specific tasks and events. Development is aimed at less predictable, long-term change and the opening up of new learning opportunities through sustained enquiry. Frustrations are most likely to be felt when development-oriented partnerships are attempted in inappropriate conditions. The distinctions between the nature and context of the two partnerships are summarized as follows:

Development partnerships	*Implementation partnerships*
Voluntary	Imposed
Informal/spontaneous	Formal/planned
Sustained/evolving	Brief events
Organic	Mechanistic
Responsive	Discharging of specified duties
Low prediction	High prediction

The next section addresses the differences between these two kinds of partnerships by comparing the various strategies of support and views of rationality and learning which they aim to promote.

Strategies for working together and models of professional learning

Taking all these problems into account, how do advisory teachers attempt to work with class teachers and what kinds of professional learning do they try to support? Recent accounts have offered possible answers to these questions. All stress the value, but also the difficulty, of collaborative enquiry.

Harland (1990) has provided a useful typology of strategies of support from participants' accounts and advisory teachers' perceptions during projects in mathematics, information technology and assessment. His four types are:

- the 'provisionary' or giving of resources mode;
- the 'hortative' or telling mode;
- the 'role modelling' or demonstrating mode;
- the 'zetetic' or enquiry mode.

Many advisory teachers in his study used three or four of these modes and sometimes appeared to use two or more simultaneously. He hints at some of the contextual constraints which forced them to change modes (lack of time, teachers' expectations and misrepresentation of the advisory teacher's function and mode of working, and headteachers' priorities), but he does not draw a qualitative distinction between them except to say that the enquiry or 'zetetic' mode is a high risk strategy which, 'when it works, can be an inspiring and productive experience for all; when it fails, it can precipitate an aggressive response which leaves the advisory teacher little option but to withdraw from the input altogether' (Harland 1990: 47). The first three modes seem to make lighter demands upon the classteachers: they are given things, told things or shown things. In the case of the enquiry mode they are asked things in order to promote reflection. This results in more, rather than less work for class teachers, and Harland found that it was not as prevalent as the other modes.

Easen (1991), in his own classification, is more explicit in judging advisory teachers' strategies. He evaluates them in relation to a particular model of teacher development, which is based upon the idea that practice will only be transformed when the 'meaning perspective' of the class teacher is transformed. He assumes that 'what teachers do about learning in the classroom seems to be a function of what they think about learning in the classroom' (Easen 1991: 88). As a consequence he argues that any approach should help the class teacher to:

- explore, clarify and 'make sense' of existing practices and value systems (otherwise the limitations of these may not be realised);
- replace the set of understandings or meanings which underpin existing practices with a new set of understandings or meanings which can guide the development of new practices;

- try out and become confident in new practices (and the concomitant value systems).

(Easen 1991: 88)

This view of learning for change is close to Mezirow's (1981) concept of 'perspective transformation', which involves the following elements:

- a disorienting dilemma;
- self-evaluation;
- recognizing that problems are shared and not exclusive to oneself;
- exploring options for new ways of acting;
- building up self-confidence and competence in new ways of acting;
- re-integration with a new perspective.

Given this developmental rather than implementation view of change processes, Easen would be unlikely to expect provisionary, hortative and role-modelling roles to yield much in terms of teachers' learning for change, especially if these approaches are used in isolation. Instead, he advocates a particular style of working in which partners can construct shared understandings and meanings about both new and existing practice. This involves a cycle of planning, action and reflection, which he suggests is the most complete approach to working and learning together for change.

Easen's strategy and Harland's zetetic mode both include enquiry, collaboration and development as the key interrelated elements. Both also recognize how difficult this is to achieve in practice. Somekh (1991) not only provides a convincing argument for the importance of collaborative enquiry, she also outlines detailed tactics for making it work. Like Easen, she espouses a model of teacher development that is built upon reflection and she describes the steps that an advisory teacher might take to help a class teacher. These steps are based upon the processes of action research, of helping the teacher to be self-questioning and open to change by analysing specific classroom interaction and situations. It is a model of teacher development and not of curriculum implementation.

This form of organic, development-oriented partnership is difficult to achieve. Its success cannot be guaranteed through a set of instant procedures. The partners need to have the resilience, especially in the early stages, to manage their participation and to understand the evolving relationship. Somekh does not assume that there are weaknesses in the teacher's practice which the advisory teacher should put right through the implementation of solutions imported from elsewhere. If lasting change is being sought, it is not sufficient for the advisory teacher to inform, demonstrate or offer resources. Day (1989) takes a similar view of 'critical friendships', which will encourage learning and autonomy in teacher appraisal schemes. He sees critical friendships as: 'practical partnerships entered voluntarily, based upon a relationship between equals and rooted in a common task or shared concern' (Day 1989: 9). Like Somekh, he argues that it is important to recognize and use teachers' capacity to be self-critical, by emphasizing reflection and discourse. Potentially, the critical friend should: 'Assist in processes of learning and change so that ideas, perceptions, values and understandings may be shared through the mutual disclosure of feelings, hopes and fears' (Day 1989: 9).

What is being proposed is a type of learning partnership which gives weight to the personal and interpretive dimensions of teachers' knowledge. Unlike technical and objective knowledge this kind of professional knowledge is largely implicit and is gained through the job of teaching. Technical and objective knowledge, however, is mainly explicit and can be learned away from the classroom by people with no experience of teaching. These two distinct views of teacher knowledge have implications for the kind of partnership needed to improve or develop it.

Somekh, Day and Easen all advocate a form of learning that takes place in the everyday working practice of the teacher, rather than being learned elsewhere and applied subsequently. It is based on Schon's (1983) concept of the 'reflective practitioner' and his claim that the teacher's spontaneous, intuitive 'knowing in action' can be transformed through reflection. This view of teaching emphasizes judgement and the interpretation of situations of uncertainty, ambiguity and uniqueness. Schon (1987: 6) refers to the way that: 'indeterminate zones of practice – uncertainty, uniqueness and value conflict – escape the canons of technical rationality'. He contends that a situation is uncertain when we cannot depend upon prior solutions, and it is unique when it defies the simple application of existing theories or techniques. Where there is a conflict of values about what to do, the choice of methods is not merely a technical task. For Schon, the indeterminate zones of practice are central to professional practice and they are handled by what he calls the practitioner's 'core of artistry'. This view is echoed by Nias (1989) and Woods (1991), both of whom stress the artistry and creativity of primary school teachers.

If advisory teachers aim to help teachers to develop their artistry rather than top up their technical knowledge, this probably requires a collaborative enquiry and development mode in the host teacher's classroom, which is sustained long enough to achieve depth, continuity and direction. However, as Harland (1990) has found, meeting these conditions is rare and difficult.

If any approaches to advisory teaching could be called easy or straight-forward, they would be those in more common use: the provisionary, hortative and role-modelling modes. They offer technical knowledge by giving, explaining or showing new things. The problem is that the advisory teachers often have to move on to the next assignment and it is the busy class teacher's subsequent responsibility to implement change through the application of the increased knowledge. This implementation approach to change relies upon the teacher's individual technical or objective rationality.

Schulman (1984), however, has warned of the limitations of individual rationality. He has used the term 'bounded rationality' to describe how personal schemata or conceptual frames are used to transform what is taught.

Simon (1965: 81) has also suggested that 'objective rationality' is not a helpful concept because it requires:

- a complete knowledge of consequences of the choice, but knowledge of consequences is fragmentary;
- imagination and anticipation of the value of the consequences, whereas values can only be imperfectly anticipated;
- choice among all possible alternative actions, but only a few alternatives come to mind.

According to Simon, people simplify the ways that they make decisions. He uses the concept of 'subjective rationality' to describe the limited and selective consideration of alternatives and consequences. In the case of teachers, it is likely that their decision-making will be limited and simplified by such factors as their expectations of students and their views of their own capabilities. Moreover, there are other reasons for doubting the notion that teaching is solely a technical-rational activity.

Nias (1989), for example, has shown how teachers' personal needs and identities influence classroom practice, and Wagner (1987) has recognized the emotional and the contradictory rather than the rational aspects of teachers' thinking. Wagner describes different types of self-generated dilemmas or 'knots' which often cause teachers to act paradoxically in classrooms.

Such attempts to understand the way teachers think lead us away from deficit models towards an appreciation of how we might build upon what teachers already know and do about teaching, rather than what they cannot do, or do not know. Desforges and McNamara (1979) and Brown *et al.* (1988) have studied teachers' professional craft knowledge, which is partly tacit and which is gained mainly from practical experience. This form of knowledge is used spontaneously and routinely in classrooms, and Zeichner *et al.* (1987) have attempted to find what influences its development in new teachers. They point to the need to understand the informal cultures of the schools as well as the tactics of formal support and control.

The study of professional craft knowledge is particularly relevant for those employed as advisory teachers, because it represents an attempt to understand the framework of concepts which have meaning for the teachers themselves. At the time of writing much of the advisory teaching in the UK is focused upon the subjects of the National Curriculum in the primary school phase. The task is to help experienced teachers, with extensive knowledge of their professional craft, to learn new subject content. As yet there is little certainty about how that might best be achieved. Schulman's (1987) use of the term 'pedagogical content knowledge' may prove to be useful because it refers to: 'that special amalgam of content and pedagogy that is uniquely the province of teachers, their own special form of professional understanding' (Schulman 1987: 8). Pedagogical content knowledge is not just a set of choices of ways of presenting the subject matter. It also involves the means of transforming that knowledge. What is of particular interest to advisory teachers is his view of how pedagogical content knowledge grows as teachers transform their subject content knowledge for the purposes of teaching.

A useful theoretical model of teachers' reasoning and action has been developed from Schulman's work. Wilson *et al.* (1987) identify six aspects of teaching in a cycle of: comprehension of subject matter, transformation of subject matter, instruction, evaluation, reflection and new comprehension. 'New comprehension' is defined as enriched understanding, enhanced with increased awareness of purposes, subject matter, self and students. One of the apparent weaknesses of such a model is the over-simplified circular sequence of discrete thinking and action that it suggests, since it seems to deny the possibility of insights occurring at unexpected times. The authors do, however, acknowledge that learning of this kind is unpredictable because: 'the enriched understanding may grow slowly by accretion. Alternatively, a single experience may promote a quantum leap. In many cases, however, no changes occur for long periods of time' (Wilson *et al.* 1987: 120).

The model offers a useful heuristic framework for groups of advisory teachers to plan and review their own approaches to supporting teachers' learning, and to decide at which point they should try to break into the circle of teachers' comprehension, reasoning and action. Taken in conjunction with Harland's typology of approaches, it suggests a series of important questions about the relationship between advisory teachers' purposes and procedures, especially in promoting the development of National Curriculum subjects in primary schools. What kind of teacher learning is possible in the hortative mode, say in a one-day conference? What kind of teacher development is being attempted in the 'role-modelling' mode, when an advisory teacher works with a whole class and the class teacher observes? What can be achieved in brief discussions? How do single events like workshops, exhibitions or displays help teachers to learn? To use Harland's shorthand, what can be achieved by a particular combination of giving, telling and showing over a given period of time?

At best, these common aspects of advisory teaching might, in Schulman's terms, assist teachers to adapt their existing ideas, to review new materials or design a new activity. They may help in the process of 'transformation' of content or contribute towards comprehension of the subject, especially if they are an integral part of a broader set of professional development activities. At worst, and especially in a 'hit and run' form, they may do little more than introduce a new topic or activity like a 'red herring' into a teacher's habitual practices.

On the other hand, the more ambitious aim – to promote Mezirow's 'perspective transformation' or Schulman's 'new comprehension' – implies a longer-term development model of change, based on experienced teachers' existing understanding. Whether their aim is to help teachers with specialist or non-specialist subject knowledge their approach should be essentially one of sustained collaborative enquiry in development-oriented partnerships.

If resources continue to be available for advisory teachers and class teachers to work and learn together for change, especially in the context of formal appraisal schemes, then it is important that those managing the projects should be aware of the relationships between various strategies of support and different aspects of teachers' learning. In particular, the advisory teachers should be given opportunities to discuss the meaning of what, why and how they do things. Conceptual understanding of the nature of their task should be given as much emphasis as interpersonal training.

I have so far tried to argue that, for contextual and conceptual reasons, we should be cautious about making generalized claims about the long-term impact of advisory teaching. The exploratory model shown in Figure 1.1, extended from the first part of the chapter, summarizes crudely the distinctions between two extreme versions of working and learning together for change. I have labelled these two extremes the development and implementation partnerships. It is not assumed that any approach to advisory teaching will fit exclusively and neatly into one category. In any case, as Harland has found, a combination of approaches is often used. The purpose of these bipolarities is to summarize the conceptual and contextual factors that need to be considered when plotting changes or locating the patterns of emphasis in specific partnerships. As well as being useful for describing relationships between visiting advisory teachers and class teachers, the model may also help a school to compare partnerships between its teachers and curriculum leaders for different subject areas during a particular period of time.

There is a limit to how far working arrangements can be modelled and planned in advance. Regardless of intentions, some imposed working relationships will achieve little in the way of long-term learning for change and they should not be kept going to the bitter end on the grounds of obligation. On the other hand, the conditions for enquiry and development may emerge unexpectedly in what began as an 'implementation-oriented partnership'. The 'development partnership' model of working is unpredictable in pace and direction, and once it is underway it should not be judged prematurely or stopped arbitrarily. Learning partnerships between teachers are not static. Given increased conceptual understanding of the task, and awareness of context, it is the judgement of those doing the work that will determine what is appropriate.

In working and learning together for change, the quest is not for more smooth-running procedures. What we need are partnerships with clearer

Figure 1.1 A model of development and implementation partnerships

DEVELOPMENT PARTNERSHIPS   IMPLEMENTATION PARTNERSHIPS

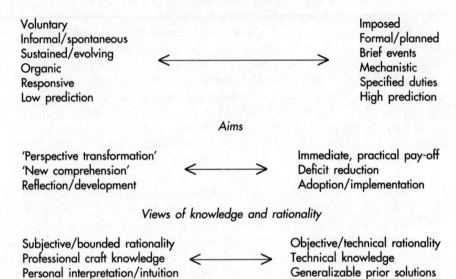

Nature and context

Voluntary   Imposed
Informal/spontaneous   Formal/planned
Sustained/evolving   Brief events
Organic   Mechanistic
Responsive   Specified duties
Low prediction   High prediction

Aims

'Perspective transformation'   Immediate, practical pay-off
'New comprehension'   Deficit reduction
Reflection/development   Adoption/implementation

Views of knowledge and rationality

Subjective/bounded rationality   Objective/technical rationality
Professional craft knowledge   Technical knowledge
Personal interpretation/intuition   Generalizable prior solutions

Emphasis in strategies

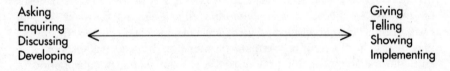

Asking   Giving
Enquiring   Telling
Discussing   Showing
Developing   Implementing

and more ambitious aims, more discretionary choice, more experimentation and better recording and communication of what happens, so that advisory teachers may learn from each other, and schools and teachers may learn to make the best use of them.

2

Preparing for school staff membership: students in primary teacher education

Robin Yeomans

Courses in primary teacher education have tended to be structured around the widely accepted assumption that being a primary teacher involves working with children in classrooms, largely in isolation from other teachers. I suggest that this assumption does not reflect teachers' experiences, and that the evolution of primary school organization over the past 20 or so years has increasingly emphasized the importance of teachers' ability to work with colleagues in school. As a consequence, teacher education courses need to reflect the complexity of the job of a primary teacher in the 1990s by preparing students for their role as staff members as well as classroom teachers. However, the task presents particular difficulties, and I want to consider some of the ways in which it can be tackled.

Collaboration is an essential part of the primary teacher's role. A child's education is shared between many teachers as that child passes through a school. A school's staff needs to ensure that children experience a coherent curriculum and that there is as smooth as possible a transition when children change classes. The belief that this could be achieved by a headteacher writing curricula and teachers following them has been exposed as a fiction (e.g. CACE 1967; ILEA 1986). As the curriculum has become more complex and the management responsibilities of heads have changed and grown, they no longer have the time or expertise to dominate the curriculum in a way that might once have seemed possible.

Following contractual changes in 1987, primary schools have moved from having a few post-holders paid an additional allowance for their expertise in specific curriculum areas to a stage in which all teachers can be asked to accept responsibility for leading their colleagues in some aspect of the school curriculum or organization. Time for collaboration no longer depends on goodwill. The teacher's working year is defined as a theoretical 1265 directed hours, including closure days for staff training and time at the end of the teaching day, supplemented by an undefined amount of non-directed time. In short, teachers can now be required to meet regularly in order to plan, learn and collaborate. They will often be led by their peers, and be asked to accept their own share of curriculum leadership.

Further, changes in staffing structure and responsibilities have been followed by reorganization of the curriculum through the Education Reform Act. Staff have been given the complex task of turning the theory of the National Curriculum into reality as part of their explicit School Development Plans.

Organizational changes apart, belonging to a primary staff has always made considerable demands on interpersonal skills. Day-to-day interaction in the unique environment of one school creates a staff culture, which is shaped by and which belongs to the particular individuals who work there. It becomes the medium in which collaboration flourishes or is discouraged. While not all primary schools are happy places (Hartley 1985), some staffs develop dominant cultures in which collaboration is valued as an experience that is rewarding both personally and professionally. Nias *et al.* (1989) have discussed the nature and origins of the 'culture of collaboration'. They suggest that a culture's main components, exemplified through and in the words and actions of its 'founders' and 'bearers', are: 'beliefs and values, understandings, attitudes, meanings and norms (arrived at by interaction); symbols, rituals and ceremonies' (Nias *et al.* 1989: 18). Using case studies of five primary schools with 'positive models of adult relationships', they argue that the culture of collaboration is built on the beliefs that:

> individuals should be valued but, because they are inseparable from the groups of which they are a part, groups too should be fostered and valued . . . the most effective ways of promoting these values are through openness and a sense of mutual security.
>
> (Nias *et al.* 1989: 47)

They further argue that this culture is consciously developed and maintained by the head and staff.

In other words, the implications of recent changes in primary staff structure, the renewed emphasis on the need for collaboration to achieve planning goals and the nature of some primary staff cultures appear to be complementary. Where a primary school's culture emphasizes individualism at the expense of collaboration, the staff are likely to find particular difficulty in responding to the expectation that their planning is collaborative and that classroom implementation is coordinated. Conversely, primary schools which have a dominant culture of collaboration may be more successful at curriculum planning.

I shall now focus more closely on staff membership, before considering how students who are intending to become primary teachers might explore the implications of being staff members.

Staff membership means more than being employed to work in a particular primary school. It is concerned with the capacity of an individual to recognize, understand, accept as legitimate and adopt the staff's culture, including the meanings that the group's rituals and symbols carry for its members as expressions of shared values and attitudes. Membership also implies that the individual has been accepted as part of the group, and that once accepted, the new member's own behaviour expresses and may shape the staff culture.

Because primary schools have relatively 'flat' hierarchies and small staffs, casual staff interaction and formal leadership and membership roles are not always easily distinguished (Yeomans 1987). There may be several leaders and forms of leadership influencing the nature of the culture which emerges. Whether an action constitutes leadership or membership may depend more on whether it sustains existing values, attitudes or beliefs or establishes new ones than on the person's position in the school's hierarchy.

Moreover, the relatively small size of primary staffs and the regular, if some-times fleeting, interactions in staffrooms and corridors mean that personal and professional concerns are seldom totally separate from each other. The affective dimension of staff relationships can confuse and be confused by professional issues and discussions, so that the person who disagrees funda-mentally with a colleague's curriculum proposals at a staff meeting may be the one who offers to take the same colleague to the dentist the following day.

Further, when it comes to collaboration on formal tasks, such as curricu-lum planning, members of a school staff depend on each other. For exam-ple, a head's proposals for change in curriculum policy are affected by the extent of teachers' willingness to respond constructively and actively. Simi-larly, the success of a structure in which all or most members are curriculum co-ordinators depends on the willingness of colleagues to accept peer leader-ship. If teachers' contracts now require that each acts as leader at some time, then this also means that each acts as a member at other times. Simi-larly while taking overall responsibility, the head also behaves as a member.

Interdependence is now a formal requirement, to the extent that 'whole-school' has become a new educational cliché. Time is allocated for col-laboration to happen, and there are tasks which require collaboration. A coherent response to the National Curriculum needs a collective staff effort, and interdependence is emphasized by the public nature of the assessment programme and reporting to parents. The requirement that schools prepare School Development Plans has turned whole-staff collaboration and planning from an optional extra into a mandated aspect of primary schools' work.

In short, the skills and understandings of collaborative adult relationships are now too important as ingredients of professional life in primary schools to be ignored by teacher educators. Yet, in the past, teachers have seldom been trained to understand the implications of their role as staff members.

There is a need to make staff membership part of the curriculum for initial teacher training. In the next section I shall consider some of the implications of doing so.

Student access to staff membership

Preparing students for staff membership presents some problems not met in preparing them for teaching children. The first is the students' own perception of the nature of the job and hence their reasons for wanting to teach. Their own experiences of school life have usually given limited access to the implications of staff membership for teachers. Students are unlikely to have considered this to be an important aspect of teaching. Even when students have been primary classroom helpers as part of their work experience before coming to college, they may not have been invited into staffrooms or admitted to planning meetings.

The second problem is that students have come to college from an educational system which has so far emphasized individual achievement rather than group achievement, and stressed competition rather than collaboration. Moreover, their qualifications show that they are the successes of that system. Any interpersonal or collaborative skills will have been incidental to that success, and will have had no formal value placed upon them. Students arrive at college to prepare for a career in which most of the working time is spent in isolation from other adults. Their suitability for such a teaching career will be assessed on their performance as individuals, with classroom performance quite rightly the main focus of that assessment.

Thirdly, having reached college and gone out on school experience, students tend to find that it is the classroom where they feel the 'self' most exposed. For this reason, classroom survival remains their understandable first concern. Being seen as a teacher from a child's perspective becomes an achievable goal because students are given the time, opportunities and most of the responsibilities of the classroom role. The same is seldom true of staff membership. Although success in the classroom may contribute to their credibility with school staff, it is not in itself a sufficient condition for staff membership. Moreover, the student's opportunities to experience membership are restricted. It is difficult to understand the meanings conveyed by the subtleties of fleeting interactions in staffrooms. In any case, the brief periods of school experience are unlikely to allow sufficient time for students to experience personally the process of acceptance as a colleague. Often students discover 'the way we do things here' by behaving inappropriately and being told they are doing so. Although some students may have access to staff planning and training meetings, they seldom have the chance to function as curriculum experts, to present a policy, or even to participate as active members in a meeting. Indeed, to attempt to do so could be to transgress a norm of student status.

Nevertheless, students do have the advantage of becoming a legitimate, accepted and natural part of most staffrooms. As students they are relatively 'invisible' and so may see, hear, learn and begin to understand how staff membership is expressed, but with the detachment of a relative outsider. They are ideally placed to be participant observers.

The best chance to experience and understand the nature of staff membership comes on final school experience, usually in the fourth year of a four-year BEd course. By then, students have worked in several schools for periods of up to five weeks, have begun to absorb something of the culture of teaching, developed some classroom skills and become more comfortable in their relationships with children. The six or seven weeks of a final school experience are sufficient for the student to become familiar with and to begin to conform to staff norms. The considerable classroom responsibility that they are given at this stage of their course means that they fulfil the teacher role largely unsupported. They may demonstrate their professional competence, become part of the day-to-day interchanges and be accepted as 'temporary' staff members. Some may become so much a part of the staff group that they are encouraged to seek jobs in the school when they have qualified. However, staffroom participation is not in itself sufficient to ensure that the nature and demands of membership are understood. Time and distance for reflection and analysis with fellow students are necessary to make sense of those experiences. Moreover, a student may have been unlucky in his or her school placement. While it can be educative to experience a situation in which staff find collaboration difficult, it is important that a student can know what collaboration felt like, albeit at second hand. By sharing their experiences of schools, final-year students can begin to develop analytical frameworks within which to organize the detail of staffroom experiences, so that they can understand the implications of their own behaviour for colleagues and begin to shape their future actions as staff members.

Valuable though final school experience is, as a single period late in a student's course it can have only a limited influence on future membership performance. Since students have only limited access to the school staff at work together, their course must also give them surrogate experiences to develop and exercise the skills of effective group membership. If collaboration can become part of the course culture, expressed through experiences on the course, as well as part of course content, it may become an accepted part of 'the way we do things as students' and ultimately as teachers.

Learning about the individual and the group

In order to prepare Bedford students to be primary staff members, they are introduced to key ideas and relevant skills. These are:

- the significance of the self in the experience of staff membership;
- the relationship between the self and the group;
- the influence of the group and its culture in shaping individual behaviour;
- the role the individual plays in maintaining that culture;
- the individual nature of each primary school's culture and the ways it is manifested through its norms, symbols and rituals.

In appreciating 'the significance of the ordinary' (Nias *et al.* 1989: 183), students can learn to understand how a school's culture is sustained through everyday behaviour and how to recognize the meanings carried by symbols. Ultimately their ability to recognize and model staff membership behaviour will accelerate their acceptance and enhance their effectiveness as staff members. Students can discover how interpersonal skills such as sensitivity, flexibility and openness in relationships with colleagues can lead to an empathy with them which enables the growth of shared understandings and makes possible effective collaboration. They are introduced to the structure of primary schools as organizations, to the complexity of the role of curriculum coordinator, to the importance of interpersonal skills in facilitating active membership when leading colleagues and in giving constructive support when others are leading.

Many of these issues are made explicit within the content of lectures, readings and directed activities. However, their significance is best understood when it is reinforced as part of the experience which students share on their course.

Structuring the experience of collaboration

In common with many other initial teacher education courses, the Bedford course seeks to achieve the development of reflective teachers by emphasizing reflection on experiences within college and school as an important course feature. This is achieved:

- by using stable groups as working units for parts of the course;
- by emphasizing collaborative reflection on tasks and experiences;
- by assigning a facilitating role to group tutors;
- by setting students collaborative tasks to complete within the course and as part of school experience;
- by making the group's processes a part of the agenda for reflection.

The size and stability of the tutorial group enables students to share an experience which imitates that of belonging to a primary school staff. As members of a group of the same 12 or 14, from different backgrounds and of varying ages, meeting for several hours each week, students experience the affective dimension common to all small task groups. Differences of perspective emerge, norms develop, and in time the group develops its own culture. The group may or may not collaborate effectively, may confront or avoid differences, and may be either supportive yet unchallenging, or critical and open. Whichever developmental pathway the group follows, it will offer its members an experience of group membership that they can use to understand the relationship between individuals and groups.

The normal procedure is that these groups spend most of their time engaged in tasks related to the particular theme under review within their course. Tasks may be carried out individually, but a regular part of each session is sharing and discussion. The process is intended to follow that described by Abercrombie (1969), in which members share perspectives on a common task, and in which they may discover that the world does not necessarily seem the same through different eyes.

Students' success in gaining insights into the uniqueness of their own perspective and in learning to understand and value the perspectives of their colleagues relies to some extent on the skills of group tutors. The tutors' chief role is to enable the group to develop and function, so that all members are able to participate and to work with silent or dominant members. Some groups may conspire unconsciously to induce their tutor to adopt a directing role, but this is to be resisted since otherwise members would tend to avoid the responsibilities of active membership, substitute passive followership and reinforce dependence on the tutor.

The time that students spend in schools is important because it provides a tangible experience of primary school cultures and of the significance of collaboration in schools' organization. Moreover, it is a safe type of experience for members to share and compare when they return from different settings. The discovery of similarities and differences in staff cultures can generate insights which may be particularly helpful for beginning teachers, especially since they can, as students, be somewhat distanced from the situations in which they participate.

In short, the course is structured so that conceptual work and first-hand experiences are mutually reinforcing. New teachers need to feel confident about becoming staff members of schools. I now turn to the college experiences that seek to achieve this end.

Experience in groups

Rather than attempting to catalogue all of the activities and experiences a group might share, I shall describe and comment on particular instances which illuminate important aspects of the learning and development of groups and individual members.

Early days in group formation

It is the first few weeks of this first-year group's course. They are predominantly female, a majority being mature students. They are already disgruntled at not being given a clearer lead by their tutor. They obediently discuss their recent visit to a nursery school. Several mature students are noticeably dominant, so that some 18-year-olds have little chance to speak. One in particular talks only when I ask her a question. Later I meet her to discuss a piece of work, and she tells me how rude and argumentative she finds her group.

The following week the group is asked to organize itself to conduct a collaborative investigation involving taking different but complementary roles in preparing a joint report. They have to decide how to share out the tasks between themselves. One sits in determined silence, two others offer competing ways of organizing the group. The tutor listens, but seems not to be helping. Another student comments loudly that it is all a waste of time and asks why the tutor couldn't say how he wanted the task done. Eventually several members opt for one of the strategies and everyone joins in with varying degrees of commitment.

Later in the week we meet again and I ask the group to think about how well it is working. One of the dominant members comments that not everyone has contributed equally to the fund of ideas. The tutor suggests that members can contribute in different ways, that all members have a right to an equal share of the group's attention, but may choose not to use it. The previously silent member then talks about how difficult she finds it to get used to the apparent violence of some of the arguments in the group, an experience she had not had at school. She confesses she was finding the mature students intimidating. In response they admit they are worried about writing essays.

Several points emerge. The newly formed group has clear expectations that tutors lead and student members follow. They feel they have come to college to be told how to be a teacher. It is understandable that they should resent a tutor who apparently does not do the job. But only by emphasizing the importance of experience can the tutor enable members to begin to explore their relationship with the group and with other individuals within it. They must negotiate how, and whether, they will collaborate. The tutor's role is to step in if difficulties become overwhelming, but by being relatively passive, he forces the group to negotiate its own roles.

Most groups are unlikely to achieve instant harmony. But once the group has worked together, however ineffectively, it has a shared history which the tutor can use to explore sensitively how roles are developing, and to help individual members decide whether they are happy with themselves and the way that the group performs. In this instance, when one member, encouraged by tutor intervention, was able to be open, others responded similarly, and members gained a clearer understanding of how everyone felt about the group.

A culture of our own

After a term together the group has heard a lecture on how groups of all sizes, including schools, classes and staffs, develop their own cultures, and how norms and values become so clearly understood that members are able to predict one another's behaviour, and the staff is able to function harmoniously with the minimum of discussion on how to proceed. Later the group is asked to consider its own culture. Members note many details – that some tend to sit in the same place and that there is clearly a tutor's chair which students always leave vacant, that everyone speaks. One student suggests that the tutor shows consideration for them, and always asks if they would like the window open, another that there is no one leader in the group. There are references to humour and to being able to pull anyones's leg. It is suggested that we all get along together, but that this isn't true of all groups.

Members have been able to identify elements of their group's culture, appreciating the relationship between group values and attitudes and the norms by which they are conveyed. They have experienced and recognized a structure in which leadership is not static, membership means taking an active part in the group's activities, and openness, albeit tinged with humour, is accepted, Finally, they confirm that collaborating professionally can be personally satisfying too. Indeed, groups regularly express the affective rewards they derive from membership by developing in their culture such rituals as end of term parties and gatherings, gifts, cards and thanks.

Testing collaboration

The tutor supports the group into its first block school experience. Students have been alerted to the importance of establishing positive relationships with staff, even though they are preoccupied with the classroom. Usually the students, working in pairs, jointly plan, organize and implement part of the curriculum for one class for two weeks. Some pairs collaborate successfully. Others find the collaboration difficult. In one classroom the teacher draws the tutor to one side and suggests they watch. In this instance three students work purposefully with two classes in a shared space, talking quietly to individuals as they move around groups working on the tasks organized for them. The student who has been leading asks the children to stop, and the other two listen while the leader ends the session. Then each checks the readiness of the groups they have been working with. In the corner is an impressive sea display, the combined product of work which different groups have done with different students.

In another classroom, one student energetically leads a class music session, while her partner looks on passively. This imbalance is becoming a feature of the relationship. At the end they and the tutor discuss the session. The active student feels she is taking an unfair share of the lead in planning and leading. Her partner agrees, but confesses to her own lack of confidence. The tutor suggests that the roles be reversed next time, but that the supporting student concentrates on giving constructive feedback to her unconfident partner.

Paired collaboration in school is a two-edged experience. Students may or may not experience the security of mutual support, but they do discover that interdependence puts responsibility on each partner in the relationship, and demands flexibility and a willingness to compromise. Some students find the relationship a difficult one to sustain, but seemingly negative experiences can produce valuable learning about one's own strengths and weaknesses.

Subsequently, the collaborative skills of the whole tutor group are retested in college.

> The activity is a thematic study. The group has now been together for six months. It has developed a culture of its own, and paired school experience has already exercised members' collaborative skills. The group has a week in which to organize itself to plan, carry out and display the products of a thematic study derived from some aspect of the local environment. Members must agree and structure a theme, assign roles, make arrangements to co-ordinate individual work and agree their timetable.
>
> The tutor offers help as needed, but the group confidently declines. Within a day a male mature student confirms to the tutor that they are to study the effects of change in the local country park, and that jobs have been assigned. During the week, conversations with various group members suggest that the same mature male is being too dominant, some members are working hard and meeting regularly, others have been inconspicuous, one has disappeared completely, and the outcome is likely to be sparse in content.
>
> By Friday morning all except the missing member (who had been ill) are gathered with their contributions. Two previously inconspicuous members bring the successful products of their researches at the record office, another contributes skilfully taken photographs of the wildlife now in the park. A sub-group has collaborated on a series of models to illustrate the change from iron age settlement, to gravel extraction, to country park. Another member offers her speculative poetry. Individuals discuss and prepare the mounting and layout of the display, seeking and receiving advice on the best alternatives. A layout plan is produced, discussed and modified as they work. Individual effort is imperceptibly coordinated and the final outcome is visually impressive and intellectually rigorous. Yet there are still students who say they can't see the point of it all.

That final comment is a reminder that some students deny the validity of experiential learning, although that very denial gives a tutor the opportunity to discuss what might have been learned. The group has recognized the need to negotiate and differentiate roles in order to achieve a complex task. Members have experienced the resentments which peer leadership can generate and the risks of being dependent on colleagues. Confirmation that trust is well-placed has reinforced group cohesion. In short, they have shared the experience of becoming a group that is able to collaborate successfully on a complex task; and they have been a team demonstrating many of the skills needed for membership of a primary staff engaged purposefully in whole-school curriculum planning.

Being a coordinator

From the beginning of their third year, students find themselves in new groups, based on the age· phase in which they choose to specialize. The junior course students are in groups of 12 to 14. Students have acquired considerable expertise in their specialist curriculum area. They have yet to consider explicitly the implications of being a curriculum coordinator, but they will do so later in the course.

> As their first major task, third-year students are split into trios, each member having a different curriculum specialism. Each trio is asked to lead a two-hour session in which they will present to their group the planning for a term's work in a junior class on a single theme, and generate discussion of issues derived from the experience of planning their theme.
> This morning's trio chooses to build language, science and art into the theme of 'communication'. They use overhead transparencies to show the pattern of pupil activity planned and the learning which might emerge for each curriculum area. Group members are encouraged to interrupt and they do so, making relevant points about other possible learning. The trio initiates discussion of how activities can be organized to take account of different abilities. Members share their previous experiences in schools, although two members have little to contribute. Afterwards the tutor tells the trio how well they had phased the session. They share their annoyance that one of the group had been absent yet again.

This activity makes considerable demands on trios. First, they have to negotiate sensitively to agree a theme that will be well-suited to each curriculum area. They need to cooperate in such a way that their individual contributions make a coherent whole. They must trust in one another's expertise and stand or fall together. Secondly, they have the problem of the session itself. Its success depends largely on their skill in leading their peers in such a way that while the trio's ideas are clearly articulated, other members feel encouraged to contribute and that their contributions are welcomed. So one mark of the trio's success is its ability to initiate new thinking in the group and ensure effective membership. Thirdly, the group may learn that all members have a responsibility. Without members' willing support, participation and readiness to accept peers' expertise, the session may be lifeless. The trio was right to identify involved participation in sessions as the minimum obligation that interdependence places on a group's members.

Seeing and perceiving

At the beginning

> A first-year group shares its recent experiences during a period of school experience. One member expresses puzzled indignation. Noticing that some of

the school's staff wore tracksuits throughout recent day visits, the student had arrived for the two weeks' experience in tracksuit trousers and an open-neck shirt. He had been called into the school office by a head wearing a suit and tie, who told him that his dress was not appropriate for a student in the school, even though some staff wore tracksuits on days when they were taking their class swimming.

The tutor suggests to the group that perhaps the head's view of what was an acceptable norm for staff members was different from his view of appropriate student wear.

At the end

Fourth-year students return from their final term in school. The experience is being dissected in the group. The subject is the contribution of the staff culture to effective functioning as a whole school. The focus is the significance of symbols and rituals in conveying shared values. Students reflect on their recent experiences and offer their perceptions. One describes the major role of a vase of flowers during changes in one primary school. A close-knit, well-established staff, with a deeply-rooted collaborative culture, was sorry to see its head leave, but anxious to continue the minor rituals which expressed their commitment to the school. One such ritual was the appearance in the school entrance every week of a fresh vase of flowers, put there by one of the most established staff, and accepted as part of the everyday scene. A new head came, and there seemed every reason to continue this custom. The flowers disappeared during the first week, and there was puzzled concern but no explanation. When events were repeated in the second week, concern became anger, expressed as the main topic of staffroom conversation. The new head had said she had removed the flowers, and didn't want them put in the entrance.

This important piece of staff history had been shared with the student in a staffroom whose members were united against its head as a consequence of that incident. The head had been in the school for a year, but now only entered the staffroom for formal meetings.

These two experiences show how easily an outsider can misperceive the meaning and significance for group members of seemingly trivial events. They also demonstrate that, given time, students can develop the sensitivity to learn to behave as, and become, insiders. They have the skills to recognize and interpret the complexities of a school culture. After all, students have a particular need to understand rapidly the workings of the staff cultures they encounter, if they are to be successful student teachers in those contexts. Their vulnerable position makes them value those schools where commitment to collaboration means that they are welcomed and supported. Moreover, having had sustained experience of several school staffs within the four years of their course, they have a ready comparison for judging each new experience of staff membership.

Summary

I have suggested that staff membership is an important part of the experience of being a teacher. Since members influence the culture they share, and since the development of a collaborative culture can make membership personally and professionally rewarding, teachers need to understand their own staff cultures. Changes in conditions of service and in the organization of primary schools have combined with the effects of the Education Reform Act on curriculum, accountability and financial management, further to affect teachers' roles. In particular, most teachers can expect to perform some leadership role in relation to their staff peers, and be required to contribute actively in whole-school planning. Thus staffs who have learnt the skills of successful collaboration are well-placed to respond to professional obligations and are likely to find staff membership personally rewarding.

If students are to become effective new teachers in the 1990s, they too need to acquire the skills associated with staff membership. School experience gives students some opportunities to understand the implications of the role. But the subtle nature of staff cultures, students' temporary positions in school, and staff and student perceptions of the student role, mean that students have only restricted time and opportunity to develop that understanding, except during the lengthy final school experience.

I have suggested that initial teacher education courses need to be structured so that they offer an alternative set of collaborative experiences in stable groups which are broadly of the size of large primary school staff groups. Tutors acting in a facilitating role can then help students to develop insights into the nature and cultures of groups and what these mean for primary staff membership. I have suggested that the key issues to be addressed are:

- the self and the group;
- the relationships between members;
- leaders and group culture;
- the nature of effective collaboration and the skills which maintain it;
- the role of the curriculum coordinator.

Finally, I have described and discussed some group experiences and suggested how these relate to a cumulative understanding of what primary staff membership entails.

The lack of subtlety of tutors' skills, the unwillingness of some students to modify their initial perceptions of what pedagogy in initial teacher education should look like, and the problems of preserving small group experiences in the face of worsening staff–student ratios, are limitations on the success of efforts to prepare students for staff membership. If students are to become flexible, open, supportive and sensitive to their colleagues and to the culture they share, and also able to participate effectively in collaborative staff planning both as leaders and as members, then didactic pedagogy is inadequate. Learning rooted in experience is more likely to be reflected in collaborative behaviour.

3

Working together: developing reflective student teachers

Kate Ashcroft

It seems uncontroversial to suggest that student teachers should have the opportunity and encouragement to reflect upon elements of their life and course during their training. When the encouragement and opportunity for such reflection come to be translated into practical terms within teacher education institutions the consensus disappears and a number of problems emerge. These problems may result from a number of sources:

- People have different ideas about what constitutes reflection.
- It is assumed that, given intelligent students, reflection will automatically take place.
- There are differences of opinion as to the best method of encouraging reflection.

To a large extent the last two problems may be a function of the first. To many teachers, students and teacher educators, reflective teaching encompasses the notion of deliberation. This somewhat limited view underlies the development of apprentice models of teacher training, such as the licensed teacher scheme. I would argue, however, for a more complex definition of reflective teaching, which includes not only deliberation but also action and values. In this chapter I shall put forward a model of reflective teaching which has implications for teaching and learning methods within initial teacher education, for the place of school-based work within such courses and especially for the role of group work of various kinds. In doing this I will give examples of ways that reflective teaching may be developed through students working together and in collaboration with teachers, tutors and parents. I shall draw on my experience in two institutions, Oxford Polytechnic and Westminster College.

Reflective teaching

The idea of reflective teaching simply as deliberation seems inadequate for a number of reasons. It gives no direction to such deliberation. Student teachers are very concerned with 'coping' in the classroom. Deliberation that is exclusively focused on such coping may lead to students falling back on teaching methods they have encountered in their own schooling. This is unlikely to be an adequate basis for a teaching career that may span four decades. In addition, the preoccupation with coping does not encourage students to examine, challenge or change their attitudes. Hogben and Lawson (1984) found that attitudes held by students at the commencement of training appear to be very resistant to change, and such changes as do occur tend largely to disappear during the first year of teaching. Zeichner and Teitelbaum (1982) found that once survival skills have become the main objective, critical thinking in the classroom is inhibited. A course based on reflective teaching should therefore aim to promote critical enquiry and encourage students continuously to examine their assumptions during the course and develop the qualities that will sustain this as a life-long activity. Such enquiry and challenge to assumptions cannot easily be done in isolation. The student needs to discover that others have ideas different from hers and to use the perspectives of others in order to ensure that her enquiry is not blinkered by her own preconceptions.

The only sure thing about education in the next century is that it will change. In any case, the range of teaching situations is so great that students cannot find the best solution to all the problems they will meet merely through the operation of 'common sense'. Teachers operate in social situations and problems cannot be solved in isolation. A course based on reflective teaching must therefore enable students to solve problems in cooperation with children and other adults.

In the past, most courses of initial teacher training were based on the premise that the student would be taught educational theory and then expected to practise it in the classroom. Carr and Kemmis (1986) point out that years of attempting to teach theory to students and then to get them to apply it have not proved very successful. Many students may have espoused the educational theory that they encountered in their colleges, but as Argyris and Schon (1974) discovered, in most cases this theory was not translated into practice, did not become 'theory in use'. It may be that one problem is a shortage of time. Students and teachers must react instantly to a number of demands as they arise. They do not have the time to translate the theory that they have studied into classroom action. A more crucial problem is that such theories usually fail to meet immediately the students' needs in the situations they encounter. They find that they cannot solve problems through the direct 'application' of theories derived from situations very different from their own. Students may then reject the notion of theory and fall back on imitation of the class teacher, though much of the subtlety of the experienced teacher's action is impossible for the student to observe directly. In addition, features such as ground rules for behaviour may be established long before the student joins the class. Even when students are placed with a successful teacher, a pure apprenticeship model may lead to the student acquiring an impoverished repertoire of action, and discourage her professional growth. A course based on reflective teaching must therefore enable students to construct their own 'theories in action':

> developing one's own continuing theory of practice under real time conditions . . . means that the professional must learn to develop micro-theories of action that, when organised into a pattern, represent an effective theory of practice.
>
> (Argyris and Schon 1974)

These theories need to be continuously reappraised and evaluated in the light of the student's growing experience in the different contexts she encounters. It seems likely that students will be facilitated in the organization, appraisal and evaluation of their developing theories of teaching through interaction with others.

Certain skills needed for teaching, such as voice control, lettering or questioning, can be directly taught. Such skills are important but not sufficient for reflective teaching. It is necessary to develop other skills, including the abilities to work as part of a team, to communicate and exchange ideas and to engage in self assessment. In addition, Zeichner and Teitelbaum (1982) point out that certain other qualities need to be developed. These include open-mindedness, responsibility and wholeheartedness.

Open-mindedness includes the willingness, and indeed desire, to seek out and examine alternative perspectives, such as those of other students, teachers, parents, children and educational researchers. An open-minded student would wish to examine critically a new educational idea or educational orthodoxy in order to discover its weaknesses. However, she would not make a 'knee-jerk' reaction and automatically reject an idea because it did not precisely fit her assumptions or the situation. Rather, she would be aware that in education there are no universal solutions, but merely those that offer particular advantages in certain situations but not in others.

Students are often concerned about 'coping' in the classroom. A responsible student would try to move away from this preoccupation and consider the long-term as well as short-term consequences of her actions. In this way she is enabled to consider not only 'what works' from her point of view or 'what the children enjoy' but also 'how worthwhile it was'. This consideration of 'worthwhileness' involves paying attention to the long-term effects on children and thus to the social, political and economic context of educational action. To achieve this she must examine with others the effects of her assumptions and actions, lest she fall into the trap of interpreting information in a way that confirms her own preconceptions and prejudices.

Wholeheartedness implies that responsibility and open-mindedness are enduring attributes of the students and not merely confined to particular situations or courses. In particular they are not assumed for the purpose of getting good grades on a course. Wholeheartedness involves the student in taking a moral stance and in continuing to review that stance.

Critical enquiry as a collaborative process

Critical enquiry is both a cause and an effect of the development of these qualities. It is a process that requires students to explore and investigate a variety of theories, perspectives, actions and consequences in relation to real situations. The classic action research cycle offers a framework for a form of critical enquiry that is practical and focused.

The process is essentially one of experimentation and evaluation. The role of the tutor is to act as facilitator to enable the experimentation and evaluation to be as informed as possible. For this reason the student teacher needs to collect information at each stage. She needs information in order to make realistic plans. Observation during action will be used to help her to try to respond sensitively and adapt her plans as she goes along. She needs to collect further information on the effectiveness of her action in order to evaluate it and make new plans. This view is of reflective teaching as a research-based activity. Through action research, students learn a variety of data collection techniques and gain a thorough understanding of practical research methods. We must, however, be cautious about the use of a classic action research model. Students find that, in practice, classroom research seldom occurs in a neat cycle. This is not because they are inefficient researchers, but rather because classrooms are complex places and any aspect of teaching that the student wishes to investigate has many facets which cannot be isolated from each other. In addition, the pace of classroom action means that plans are modified long before the cycle is completed, and much planning, reflection and observation must occur simultaneously. The cycle is useful, though, in indicating the necessity of addressing all stages and in stressing the importance of systematic data collection. Data collection does not apply exclusively to numerical data of the sort normally resulting from observation schedules, although these have their uses, but also to more qualitative data, such as 'fly on the wall' observation, discussion with children, audiotape transcripts and the student's record of her thoughts and feelings. These provide a record which can then be the focus for more leisurely reflection, planning and group discussion.

An experienced teacher wishing to collect data on, for example, children's attitudes to school, may be aware of an efficient method and the type of questions she might ask. A student, on the other hand, may well need help with this type of planning. First, she will need to decide more exactly what it is she wants to find out and for what purpose. Then she will need to plan a means for uncovering this information. Quite often this plan may take the form of a loose script for a learning conversation with a child or a group of children. In the early stages students often assume that the most useful questions will occur to them in the course of the conversation, with the result that impoverished data result. The college learning group can play a useful role here. Students can share ideas on what aspects should be central to the investigation, what might constitute 'good' questions or what other methods there are to collect relevant information.

Some information can be collected by the student as she works with children in the classroom, but much cannot, because she is often unaware of aspects of her behaviour or that of the children. Information that is particularly likely to challenge her preconceptions is often collected more readily by an independent observer. It seems important to emphasize the role of others in helping the teacher research her teaching and the classroom situation.

Similarly, many teachers are surprised when they take up a new post to discover how much they learn in a very short time. Previously they may have been unaware of the gaps in their knowledge. It is hard to know what one does not know! The classic action research model does not deal adequately with this problem. Teachers are assumed to be in a position to define all their own goals with little outside help. In the course of the research, experienced teachers may become aware of other issues which need investigation, but this is a chance rather than an inevitable consequence of the operation of the model. In the case of student teachers, with their relative inexperience of the factors that contribute to classroom problems, this difficulty will be more acute.

In all of this, the role of others, whether in groups or as individuals, becomes essential. Alternative problems or ways of conceptualizing the problems that are recognized can be drawn to the student's attention. Students need to find out about teaching and children from first-hand experience in order to create meanings for themselves. They cannot simply apply second-hand theories, a fact which often makes them reject such theories and see teaching in purely intuitive terms. However, this does not mean that they have to rediscover for themselves all the knowledge available about teaching and children. What is needed instead is a sensitive intervention by others at the right moment. This may not be a direct feeding of information, but may take the form of a question, in answering which the student realizes that she needs to find particular information herself. Equally, group work with other students can enable a student to broaden her perspective or reconceptualize her problem.

The classic action research model therefore provides useful insights and

methods for the initial education of teachers, though it must be adapted to
the particular needs of students and the reality of the classroom situation.
It must also be supplemented by sensitive intervention by tutors and teachers
and by the opportunity for group work in the classroom and group discussion
outside the school. Students need tools to solve problems, but they also
need the opportunity to investigate apparently non-problematic classroom
and social phenomena for their own sake, to deepen their understanding of
the context of education.

School experience: learning through partnership

Many teachers seem to feel that initial teacher education still emphasizes the
acquisition of theory to the detriment of practice. This has led some teachers
and politicians to welcome the advent of the licensed teacher scheme and
to hope that it may eventually develop into the main route into teaching.
The argument is that teaching is an essentially practical activity and should
be learned 'on the job'. I would argue that this notion is misconceived. This
is not to say that initial education for teaching should not be firmly rooted
in the reality of the classroom; very much to the contrary. However, reflective
student teachers need time: time to explore the ideas of educationalists
separated from them in time and space; time to explore the context of
education; time to explore the perspectives of teachers, children, peers and
parents; time to investigate and collect data on the consequences of their
actions; above all time to explore and challenge their own preconceptions
with the help of others. Licensed teachers, responsible for a class of children for most of the time, perhaps with some *ad hoc* INSET support, will
not have the time, context and opportunity for such in-depth exploration.
They may be tempted to grab ideas wholesale from hurried staffroom
consultations between lessons or from the INSET provision. What they may
be offered is a nineteenth-century apprenticeship model without the time
necessary for critical enquiry.

At Westminster College, during first block school experience, students are
assigned to schools in groups of four or six and to classes in pairs. This
provides opportunities for learning of a kind that the licensed teacher or
traditional 'teaching practice' situation cannot offer. Students can share
perspectives and discoveries about the school and the children. They will
all have experienced similar situations and events. This enables them to
share their interpretations and analyses in a much more meaningful way,
and to discover that witnesses to the same event will have very different
perspectives on it. In addition, they can act as non-threatening observers
and data collectors for each other. Such peer group involvement in school
experience enables a more enquiry-based format to be developed, in which
students are not expected to 'apply' what they have learned in college, but

rather to draw on that experience to provide a context for their enquiry into the teaching situation, the children's learning and their own action and reaction. This becomes more possible with the involvement of others: fellow students, tutors and class teachers.

The support of the class teacher is central to student teachers' learning from practical experience. The class teacher provides expertise in practical teaching skills and in understanding children's learning. She or he is often able to help, guide and inform the student on these vital matters.

Students need tutors and fellow students to further their development in the same way that children need teachers and classmates, but just as the parent is the child's prime educator, the class teacher is often the student's. Many colleges are recognizing this fact and entrusting more of the practical education of students to class teachers. Initial teacher education could not progress without the time and effort that is given freely by teachers and schools. Many take great pride in their induction programmes for students and some schools have a teacher who is nominated to be responsible for student teachers within the school. In the past, many colleges, while grateful for this help and recognizing its worth, gave the teachers little in return. This was seldom because of an unwillingness to do so, but more often because funds were unavailable. Some colleges have begun to offer teachers who are taking this increasing responsibility for the education of the next generation of teachers some in-service training for the role. This is to be welcomed. With the introduction of local management of schools, governing bodies are likely to look at the cost and benefits of non-required activities. Schemes which link the development of students with that of experienced teachers will clearly have benefits for both parties.

Westminster College has taken this idea of partnership with schools a stage further. Schools have been offered the opportunity to become link schools. Such schools are heavily involved in the education of the students during both serial (day visits) and block school experience. The teachers within those schools are offered training and thus enabled to become familiar with the role of school experience within the course and skilled in the support of students who are engaged in enquiry in their classrooms. This enables them to take on some of the work that was previously the province of college tutors. In return, consortia of schools are being offered up to ten days free INSET tuition from the college. Alternatively, individual schools can take up an offer of a one-day course within their school or a 'free ticket' for a member of their staff on a longer course. All teachers in the link school scheme become members of the college, in the same way as the students, with free access to learning, social and sports resources. The scheme enables both class teachers and college tutors to make the maximum use of their particular areas of expertise and to begin to feel a real partnership.

Serial and block school experience are organized as far as possible to enable individual students and the college to build long-term relationships and understandings with particular schools. Serial school experience is arranged so that students concentrate on children and their development in the earlier stages of their course, moving on to focus on pedagogic issues and the investigation of the wider professional context in a later stage.

The BEd team at Westminster College is considering a pilot project for the final year of the course to be school-based. By this time students will have experienced curriculum input in all main areas, been introduced to pedagogic issues and experienced block and serial school experience.

The idea is that after a brief orientation period at the start of the fourth year, students will be placed in schools, two to a class. They will be released to undertake college-based tuition and preparation and for group discussion. Teachers will be brought into the programme in an extension of the existing partnership. During their school-based work students will, under the guidance of their class teachers, divide their time between observing their partner teaching, team teaching with their partner, teaching the class observed by their partner, collecting other data in the classroom and about the school, and planning and reflection. The content of the course will cover issues normally dealt with through college-based work, such as issues of race and gender, relationships with parents and the role of the curriculum specialist. In investigating these issues in relation to a real context, it is hoped that students will be enabled to see their relevance and will acquire a broader vision of the educational debate. Students will also undertake specific reading, observation and other data collection tasks, which they will integrate into a structured learning log. This is expected to look very different from the traditional teaching practice file. An issue of importance to the student will be explored in more depth and with more rigour during the final term and will constitute the special study. Students will undertake specific assignments that are compatible with the action research model with and on behalf of the school; these will meet criteria for teaching competence. Within this model students would be enabled, with the help of teachers, to become active and continuing learners and teacher researchers, qualities which we believe will be essential for reflective teaching in a time of change.

It is not suggested that college tutors should have no role within school-based experience. The class teacher has particular skill and expertise in teaching and a deep understanding of the children in her care. The concerns of college tutors in this system should be different, but none the less relevant to the practical teaching context. They must be to help the student relate the practical context to wider pedagogic, social and educational issues. Tutors can help the student place the school experience in relationship to the rest of the course and to contexts separated from the student by time and space. In so doing they can help to ensure that the student is enabled to develop understandings and skills, to develop as a good class teacher not only 'in this school at this time', but also in the wide variety of educational situations that she may find herself in during a long career. The way to achieve both these goals is through critical enquiry.

The role of peers in promoting students' learning should also be recognized. Students can act as non-threatening observers, they can challenge interpretations, they can help each other gain insights by being a naive audience for each others' explanations and evaluation. It is as facilitators of critical enquiry that the roles of the student, tutor and the class teacher come together in the education of the next generation of teachers.

Using student groups in college-based work

The role of the class teacher becomes ever more complex. Many of the skills she needs are those required for middle or senior management in commerce or industry. She must manage the productive work of some 30 individuals, assess their interests, evaluate and implement priorities and involve them in decision-making. In addition, she will work with a variety of other adults in a number of roles, for instance as a member of the group, curriculum leader, co-professional, counsellor and provider. She must manage a complex operation within very tight resources. All this must be achieved at a time of rapid development and change. Each change must be evaluated and implemented in the best interests of the children and the school.

Students must therefore develop a variety of skills. These include time and resource management, independent learning, research, a wide variety of communication and, perhaps most importantly, interpersonal skills. Students need to be enabled to teach peers and to assess themselves and peers as well as children. Crucially, they must explore their own viewpoints and those of others.

The curriculum, assessment and pedagogy of teacher education courses also need to reflect these priorities. It has been argued elsewhere that critical enquiry, with its emphasis on the exploration of a variety of perspectives and of the notion of 'worthwhileness', seems to be a highly appropriate method for developing these skills (Ashcroft 1987; Ashcroft and Tann 1988; Ashcroft and Griffiths 1989). Initial teacher education institutions which have been examining teaching and learning methods that facilitate critical enquiry have stressed the importance of group work.

In order for students to investigate the viewpoints of others and to take them seriously it is necessary for them to work in groups, although by itself this is not sufficient. The topics discussed by the group may not reveal individual viewpoints because they may not be sufficiently emotionally engaging. The tutor may control the discussion so that only 'safe' opinions are aired. The students may feel inhibited from expressing their true feelings in front of a tutor. These problems may be overcome if the situation for group work is sufficiently challenging, the product of group work is built into the assessment system or the context allows real feelings and dilemmas to be revealed. Group problem-solving activities involving real-life conditions are likely to produce the conditions for critical enquiry. Creating this context requires particular skills on the part of the tutor, especially the ability to work alongside students as equals and, once the situation is set up, to trust them to learn from each other, often without intervention.

The BEd tutorial team at Oxford Polytechnic has developed a variety of teaching, learning and assessment methods within the college-based component of the course in order to facilitate critical enquiry and the development of prerequisite skills (see Isaac and Ashcroft 1987). From the first term of the course students engage in first-hand research and are required to work as a group in order to produce a group case study report. They are responsible for determining the criteria for assessment and for grading the work themselves. The process involves them in independent learning, peer management and negotiation. Many students find it stressful and difficult, but others are encouraged to take real responsibility for their own and others' learning. At various points during the course, students are also involved in peer teaching and peer and self assessment.

The tutorial team at Westminster College has taken some of these ideas further. The existing course handbook described the BEd as being based on the concept of the reflective practitioner. However, it became apparent that there was no agreed definition among the team as to what were the qualities of the reflective practitioner. The team spent time discussing this and came up with an operational definition that did not explicitly draw on Zeichner and Teitelbaum (1982), but that had many features in common. They decided that such a teacher is skilled in critical enquiry and is adaptable and self-motivating. In addition students should develop attributes necessary for any career which involves working with people.

These attributes were defined as follows:

1 Skills
   - skills of independent and collaborative learning;
   - interpersonal skills;
   - skills of self-assessment and self-awareness;
   - communication skills;
   - decision-making skills;
   - research skills;
   - skills of application and implementation.
2 Values
   - respect for the viewpoints of others;
   - desire to understand the viewpoints of others;
   - commitment to human values;
   - willingness to consider the long-term consequences of action;
   - willingness to enquire and research with rigour.

3 Understanding
- understanding of cultural diversity;
- understanding of the interdependent nature of human society;
- understanding of the problematic nature of knowledge;
- understanding of the student's own abilities, attitudes and needs;
- awareness of responsibility and accountability.

It was decided that all aspects of the course, subject study as well as professional studies, should be explicitly directed at fostering these skills, values and understandings. This was a crucial point, because it enabled the team to consider the holistic development of the student and because it required every aspect of the roles and responsibilities of tutors, students and teachers, and the curriculum and assessment scheme, to be reassessed.

Efforts were made to broaden the students' understandings beyond their immediate experience. Assessment tasks were acceptable if they were learning experiences in their own right, but not if they merely tested students' understanding of the taught course. New forms of assessment were introduced which emphasized the complex skills teachers need in order to work effectively as part of a team. These included group practical examinations where groups of students had to plan and implement an 'in-service' session for non-specialist peers on an aspect of their curriculum specialism.

Group tasks were designed to develop a range of observational and research techniques and include research-based assignments into students' and others' actions and perspectives. The dissertation element of the course is group-focused and workshop-based, with groups of students researching in common areas and sharing methods, criticism, data and analysis.

It was felt to be essential that students should develop skills in communication, self and peer evaluation and support if they were to work as effective team members. The assessment scheme was therefore changed to provide opportunities for self and peer assessment (structured formative assessment in the early stages) and for displaying a variety of communication skills, such as presentation using dramatic, visual and cinematic means.

Many students appeared to take an instrumental view of their assessment and learning, and were not therefore willing to consider the long-term consequences of their actions. To discourage this utilitarian attitude, a large proportion of coursework is now required but not formally assessed. The burden of assessed work has been cut by half, in order to enable the students to have more time for reflection and to encourage a greater degree of rigour in analysing and making links between the various parts of the course. Students are encouraged to focus within groups on the selection and collection of evidence; this has become an important criterion for assessment. The team felt that examinations tested a small range of the required skills and therefore the proportion of examination to coursework has been reduced.

The advent of the National Curriculum and revised criteria from the Council for the Accreditation of Teacher Education (CATE) meant that further issues had to be addressed. Among those which staff found most difficult were the introduction into the curriculum of:

> The values and the economic and other foundations of a free and civilised society in which pupils are growing up, and the need to prepare pupils for adulthood, citizenship and the world of work.
>
> (DES 1989a: paragraph 6.1)

Tutors viewed this provision with suspicion, but with staff development activities and discussion came to see its potential if offered for the development of students. It gradually became clear that the CATE requirements gave students the opportunity to discuss education within its economic, social and political context and to enquire deeply into moral questions. In addition the involvement of industrialists widened the perspectives of the students. The most positive aspect of the new provision was the development of an understanding of the importance of team-building and of methods to allow this to happen. For example, a group of students organized two INSET sessions for the tutorial staff on this. Specific team-building exercises and the systematic analysis of them are now built into many aspects of the course.

Conclusions

The teacher for the twenty-first century will need to be adaptable and equipped with a variety of higher order management and interpersonal skills. She will need to understand herself and others, be able to assess new developments and evaluate action in a very sophisticated way, and be a self-motivated, life-long learner. The preparation for this highly skilled and complex role is a major challenge for teacher educators today. Teaching is no longer, if it ever was, merely a matter of transfer of learning from the teacher to the taught.

This complexity requires the development of new ways of educating students as teachers. I have argued that a simple apprenticeship model cannot achieve the necessary objectives. What is needed instead is the development of methods to enable students to experience the process of critical enquiry with increasing rigour, so as to enable them to research educational problems and the classroom context and to become effective decision-makers. The role of collaboration is central to this process. Students need to develop appropriate skills, values and understandings through working together: for instance, through case study, peer teaching, peer assessment and organizing events.

None of this is easy. Often the process is painful, as teachers, tutors and students have to come to a deeper understanding of their roles, attitudes and assumptions, and to change aspects of each. Learning with others and through enquiry and investigation is more rigorous and uncomfortable than 'being told', but is likely to be more meaningful and to lead in the long run to greater adaptability. Such learning requires new relationships between tutors, students and teachers and between college and school. These changing relationships may be difficult in the early stages and misunderstandings may arise. However, it is my belief that these problems must be overcome if teachers are to have an initial training worthy of the twenty-first century.

Part II

The subjective experience of
changing with others

4
Reflections on a head and deputy partnership

Penelope A. Campbell

Steve and I worked together for less than a year. He was a recently appointed headteacher. I was his new, and temporary, deputy. In some ways we could hardly have been more different, in others scarcely more similar. Our professional histories differed in almost every respect. Yet our principles sprang from the same root – a deep and personal Christian faith – and, importantly, were interpreted similarly in our day-to-day relationships. Steve's intention was that we work together to formulate and begin to put into action a development plan that would give new direction to the school. What follows is a case study of our partnership as we sought to do this. It is drawn from research into school development which I conducted, as a teacher researcher, for my MA dissertation (Campbell 1989). The data used are semi-structured interviews with Steve, other staff members, the previous headteacher and myself, and documents arising from the programme of school development. A colleague on the MA course interviewed me. I conducted all the other interviews. My partnership with Steve was never intended as a focus for my dissertation. Nevertheless, the data provide rich evidence of the ways in which we worked together and a little of what we learned as we did so. In particular they show the effect we had upon the relationships of those within the school and upon its organization and management.

This chapter (read and agreed to by Steve) chronicles our partnership. It is not the full, but it is the main story. First, I describe our professional backgrounds and the history of the school in which we worked, highlighting some of the dilemmas we each faced as we came to terms with the differences between our own values and those prevailing within the school. Secondly, I describe some of the informal and formal ways in which we worked together, the programme of school development that we planned and

implemented and the effects that were evident within the school. Thirdly,
I consider what made it possible for us to work together to bring about
change. Finally, I draw some tentative conclusions about working and
learning together for change.

Steve was educated at a public school. Two terms spent helping at a
preparatory school before he went to university to take a degree in
mathematics confirmed his intention to teach. He took a PGCE course,
encountered a reluctance to allow students with a public school background
to do their teaching practices in state schools and, 'with some difficulty',
persuaded the placements tutor to allow him to go to a grammar school. His
first appointment was at a small, 'fairly formal' grammar school where he
stayed until it closed four and a half years later. Wanting comprehensive
experience and, after his marriage, a move out of London he applied for a
post in an 11–16 village college. During his seven and a half years there he
discovered that he 'wasn't really a maths teacher at all'. He became head of
year, fulfilling his pastoral role with great satisfaction, particularly as he
increasingly involved parents in discussions about their children's concerns.
He was considered 'fairly formal and fairly strict', requiring high standards
of dress and behaviour from his pupils. He was encouraged by the head to
seek promotion. When the deputy headship of St Thomas Middle School,
which has close connections with the cathedral choir (Steve was a chorister),
was advertised, applying for it 'seemed the right thing to do'. He was appointed in April 1985. In December 1986 the headteacher retired. During
the following term Steve was acting head and was permanently appointed
as the new headteacher from April 1987.

From a direct grant grammar school I went to a college of education
where I took a four-year BEd course. My first appointment was in a multi-
ethnic 9–13 middle school which, until comprehensive reorganization, had
been a junior school. It retained a primary ethos, even fourth-year pupils
spending the majority of their time with class teachers. My second appointment, as year coordinator and head of humanities, was in a purpose built,
open plan middle school in a London overspill area where a cross-curricular,
team-teaching approach was encouraged. I found both pastoral and curricular responsibilities challenging and fulfilling. From here I was seconded to
do an Advanced Diploma and shortly afterwards was appointed as second
deputy to another middle school, purpose built and semi-open plan, with
a curriculum based on 'areas of experience'. While there I began a part-time
MA and was also seconded for a term to write a report on school development
plans (Campbell 1987). Following this I joined the staff at St Thomas, on a
temporary exchange basis, in September 1987.

St Thomas Church of England Voluntary Aided Middle School (9–13 years)
is located in a small, attractive country town and has close links with the
cathedral. Created through comprehensive reorganization in September 1972,
it opened with three out of the four years and occupied the boys' grammar

school buildings. The Reverend Selwyn Wyatt was appointed as headteacher. Five of the original staff were inherited from the boys' grammar school. Of the other ten the majority had taught only in secondary schools. There was a desire, particularly among the staff who had taught at the grammar school, to maintain that status, in reputation if not in fact, and this influenced the organization of the new school. A 'careful structure' was developed, the Reverend Wyatt said. The children and staff were organized into year groups, each with four classes. In their first year pupils spent a proportion of time with their class teacher but the curriculum was generally taught through eight timetabled periods a day based on subject specialisms. Some teaching groups were set by ability. There were yearly examinations. Each pupil belonged to one of four houses.

A recognizable hierarchy existed. Authority was perceived as coming from the headteacher and was symbolized, perhaps, by Selwyn Wyatt's wearing of a gown. He was regarded as a 'paternalistic but benevolent person who made all the decisions and expected that those decisions would be carried out in a certain way' (teacher). The deputy head's role was to identify with the head in his decisions, while year leaders, who had a primarily pastoral function, played an important role in communicating policy to the rest of the staff. Curriculum post-holders either operated independently of their colleagues (teaching music to all classes, for example) or influenced colleagues in the teaching of that area of the curriculum for which they held an overall responsibility (when class teachers taught the younger pupils English, for example). Regular staff meetings, year leaders' meetings, year team meetings and curriculum meetings were held. Although Selwyn Wyatt regarded staff meetings as a means of consultation, their formality – everyone was addressed by title, for example – prevented some teachers from expressing opinions.

St Thomas was regarded by those within and without as 'traditional' and 'formal', an image reinforced by the appearance, behaviour and achievements of the pupils. Uniform was worn. Discipline was 'strict', even regimented, the consequences of misbehaviour predictable. Punishments and rewards were based on order marks, detentions, special mentions in assembly and house points. Excellence was pursued and high expectations were held of pupils academically, culturally and on the sports field. The pupils' successes were the teachers' rewards.

Underlying the organizational structures and the accepted norms of behaviour were strongly held beliefs and values associated with the Christian foundation of the school. Termly eucharists were held for each year group and for the whole school. The school itself was seen as a community within which a regard for people was fostered by an emphasis on courtesy and respect for authority. Pride in and loyalty towards the community was encouraged and the individual's contribution to corporate achievement was valued.

Over the years Selwyn Wyatt sought to maintain both the structure and reputation of the school by appointing 'older staff'. However, he also wished the school to be challenged and saw the role of deputy as important in this respect. Four deputy heads were appointed during his headship, all from outside the middle school system in the belief that they would provide new perspectives for development. The last of these was Steve.

Steve shared with Selwyn Wyatt a belief in the central importance of caring to the educational process. This was a factor in his appointment: 'It's the human being that I look for. He's got a deep humanity, a deep caring' (Selwyn Wyatt). Within a short time, however, Steve found himself with doubts about some of the norms of civility, instruction and improvement that defined the school's general character (Bird and Little 1986). At first these expressed themselves in a sense of unease about aspects of the children's behaviour (holding doors open, standing when an adult entered the classroom, moving aside when he walked down the corridor), acts which he did not object to in themselves, but which seemed excessive and a result of repeated training rather than genuine consideration. Although he found the children 'approachable' and 'chatty' and the staff friendly and supportive his feeling of unease persisted.

> *Steve*: There was a strange contradiction in my mind. In what was basically a very happy school there were certain elements which somehow weren't quite right. It was a bit like reading *Watership Down* and finding a perfectly ordered rabbit warren where you couldn't work out quite why they all put up with it, seemed happy and did as they were told.

As he got to know the school better Steve's discomfort increased. He discovered things that were at odds with his own values. There was 'a great unwillingness to be honest about what was going on', 'one couldn't admit that there was anything that wasn't quite right'. There was 'a very definite desire to cover up if there was any trouble of any sort'. A believer in the partnership between parents and teachers, Steve found it impossible to accept that parents were not involved in discussions about pupils' problems. So far was he out of step with Selwyn Wyatt on these matters that he 'led a bit of a double life for a while'. Steve's views on discipline also differed from those current within the school. He believed that Selwyn Wyatt wanted a deputy who would maintain 'strict order': 'He used to bemoan the fact that I wouldn't shout at children and eventually took to doing so himself because I wouldn't' (Steve). He also believed that the staff's expectations of his disciplinary role were disappointed in his fulfilment of it: 'They would send me a child expecting me to shout at it and send it back, and I would sit it down and have a chat and this wasn't at all what was expected or wanted.' It seems clear that although Selwyn Wyatt and Steve agreed on the principle of caring they were not agreed on its interpretation in practice.

Neither did they share the same views on the development of the school. Steve felt that planning for the future was founded on a concern to maintain present practice. Developments occurred 'piecemeal' and depended on individuals. When those individuals left the school the benefits of their initiatives were frequently lost. He came to believe that there was no encouragement to develop because no thought was given to the overall direction of development. He was frustrated in his attempts to talk with Selwyn Wyatt about longer term developments. He also felt that staff were isolated from their professional colleagues in other schools, rarely attending INSET courses. He suspected this was a 'fairly deliberate policy'.

Reflecting on his first months at St Thomas, Steve was aware that his description might be a misrepresentation because of the strength of his own affective response to the disjunction he felt between his own values and those of colleagues, in particular his headteacher. Probably Steve's strength of feeling contributed both to his conviction that change was needed and to his determination to find ways of encouraging development. Thus his immediate priority, once appointed as head, was to appoint a deputy who would help to formulate a development plan and to 'put at least the first part of that plan into action' (extract from letter to prospective applicants for the post of deputy head). At the same time he was trying to reduce tensions in the staffroom, where internal disputes were causing difficulties. Some of the conflict was related to the hopes and fears raised by his permanent appointment.

> *Steve*: My term as acting head had been marvellous because everyone had been so nice and so helpful, but as soon as I was head there were those who felt that I was going to change everything overnight and wouldn't that be marvellous and there were those who were afraid that I was going to change everything overnight and wouldn't that be terrible.

These difficulties reinforced his view that 'the only way forward was to find some way of devising this development plan'. He now included within that concept the notions of 'whole school' and 'whole staff'.

Coincidentally, during this same term I had been writing a report on school development plans (Campbell 1987). This, together with other considerations, led the governing body to invite me to join the school as acting deputy for a year. Not without some doubts I agreed to do so.

My doubts related to the differences I perceived between my educational philosophy and experience and that which I guessed to be common among the St Thomas' staff. On my first visit I found the school environment, despite its mature and lovely grounds, depressing: long, concrete corridors and flights of stairs barren of children's work; cellular classrooms with furniture organized in such a way that the predominant style of teaching was clearly didactic; closed doors; no opportunity to see how children were being taught since they rose to their feet as soon as we entered; a house system, a prefect system, a punishment and rewards system which I intuitively felt I would dislike; a timetable which, to one committed to a mainly cross-curricular, class-based approach, looked very much like a straitjacket. After listening to my description of the school, my interviewer said: 'It sounds as if there was a culture in the school that was totally alien to your way of thinking, way of being.' He was right.

So why did I agree to the proposal? I think, because of Steve. We spent that first exploratory visit watching one another and trying to divine what the other was watching for! Several things emerged from this encounter. First, we shared similar attitudes towards children.

> *Penny*: I liked the head very much. He was a very gentle person. I liked the way he treated children when I saw him around the school, the way he talked to them, and I liked the fact that when he took me round the school he was watching me to see how I acted with the children as well.

Secondly, he appreciated that I would feel uncomfortable with certain accepted organizational and pedagogical practices within the school. Although we were not entirely of one mind with regard to these, it seemed that we would be able to talk openly about our differences. Thirdly, he apparently believed that I could help him achieve his desire to formulate and implement a school development plan. I felt that we could work together. 'I felt enough in accord with him, even though I wasn't with the school, to take a chance on it' (Penny). That sense of accord underpinned my working relationship with Steve, never deserting me even when we argued about the way forward. It was strengthened perhaps because we were each prepared to accept the differences that existed between us.

I believe our working partnership effected change within the school in two main ways. The first was not so much unintentional as unstated and arose from a mutual recognition of shared values. The second was the result of a purposeful programme of school development, about which we talked at length and for which we consciously laboured.

First, then, we had an effect on the nature of the teacher–pupil relationships within the school. From the early days of Steve's appointment as deputy he had established a more personal approach to his relationships with children than had been common, an approach typified in the following account. 'When the previous deputy used to walk down the corridor all the miscreants at the other end would disappear from view, whereas when I walked down the corridor they all came rushing up to have a chat.' (Steve) I also valued a personal approach to relationships with children, believing that this affected the ethos of the school and the success of the educational endeavour. I made symbolic changes in the organization of the deputy's office, hanging curtains at the windows, putting a rug on the floor, opening the double doors wide, displaying pictures and pieces of writing that children gave me. Children began to come to the office to talk, to offer help, because it provided them with a quiet place to continue with work that had captured their interest and imagination. Thus both Steve and I consciously, though independently, modelled a particular approach to teacher–pupil relations, acknowledging children's individuality, recognizing their concerns and encouraging them to take responsibility for their own actions. However, some staff viewed our attitude with suspicion. They disliked children having access to the administrative block, believing that it gave a bad impression of the school to visitors. They believed that the nature of our relations with the children led to indiscipline. Steve and I both acknowledged that a discipline problem existed. I, and others, explained this with reference to the differences between Steve and me, and Selwyn Wyatt and his previous deputy.

> *Penny*: As I began to understand it, they'd had a very authoritarian head and this very strict disciplinarian as a deputy and, suddenly, they had a head and a deputy who talked to children on a very egalitarian basis compared with what had gone on before . . . . You'd got a complete change of style . . . . Once you took away that authoritarian lid the children just boiled over.

The difference was to do with principle, not just with personality. Neither of us was prepared to act in any other way.

> *Penny*: I think the way the fourth years particularly have behaved this year has been a direct consequence of the way Steve and I have acted, but *I still don't think it's wrong* and I think, once children are used to a new and different regime they will actually settle down. [Emphasis added.]

> *Steve*: There are aspects where I wish things were better than they are and I'm sure that if we keep working away in the way we are they ought to become better. Maybe they never will, but *I'm not going to achieve it by any other means*. [Emphasis added.]

Steve recognized, as I did not, that our attitude created ambiguity. 'It's been very hard work on the shop floor', said one teacher who went on to describe the dilemma she felt as she balanced a desire for 'strict discipline' based on 'fear of somebody at either the deputy's or the head's position' against her admiration for the personal care that pupils were receiving. Another said:

> You can always agree with the principle of what Steve does without actually going wholeheartedly along with how it works out in practice . . . . He tries to get people to come to terms with discipline and responsibility problems for themselves.

In short, the ways in which Steve and I behaved towards children challenged the tacitly accepted authoritarian foundations of teacher–pupil relationships. Yet we acted independently, in accordance with our own personal beliefs, and did not discuss the possibility of deliberately cooperating in order to bring about a school-wide change in adult–child relationships. Nevertheless, we each recognized, in the other's attitudes and behaviour, our shared beliefs and were aware of working in harmony. This made it possible for us to work together towards the same ends without finding it necessary to discuss either means or ends.

The second main effect we had was directly attributable to the programme of school development. This we both regarded as the focus of our working partnership. We each had some appreciation of the difficulties we faced. Steve's understanding was practically based, derived from his knowledge and experience of the school. Mine was theoretically based, strongly influenced by, in particular, the writings of Bolam (1984, 1986), Campbell (1985), Christensen *et al.* (1983), Fullan (1982, 1986) and Hall and Loucks (1978). Steve had already encountered the concerns of staff members over anticipated change. I was familiar with the view that the intention to involve teachers in producing and operating a plan for development actually represented an attempt to improve underlying problem-solving processes (Bolam 1986) and had recognized that this might 'be uncomfortable or threatening for staff unused to consultative procedures or the attendant responsibilities' (Campbell 1987).

The programme of school development as it evolved fell into three parts, each corresponding to one term in the school year. The first saw a series of what we felt were false starts; the second, a planned and intensive programme of professional development; the third, structured staff discussions leading to recommendations on organization, resources and staffing for the following academic year.

The first false start occurred on an in-service training day at the start of the school year. Steve decided that the staff should discuss assessment and reporting. Looking back on that meeting, he said: 'Nothing stemmed from that day at all . . . . The only person developed, I think, was me because I learned that it wasn't as easy as I thought it was going to be.' At the time, all Steve knew was that the meeting had not achieved what he had hoped. No decisions had been reached, no changes made. A year later he could reflect:

We couldn't do it because none of the mechanisms for developing anything were there, from the essential one of staff knowing how to talk to each other in real, down to earth curriculum or educational terms onwards. There wasn't the mechanism for doing anything on a whole-school basis. The only tool we had were full meetings at which one or two made the running as far as talking was concerned, and that wasn't a way to start developing things.

From this meeting onwards, I became involved in the planning. The discomfort which, at times, we both felt did not prevent us from working together, as the following extract from Steve's interview suggests:

Steve: From here on I think your input influenced considerably what I thought and what happened.

Penny: Not always comfortably.

Steve: No. Not always, because, well, I didn't always agree with you . . . . On the other hand, the basic things that I think you guided me through were the absolute essential of finding out what priorities were in people's minds, not just deciding for myself what the priorities were.

In November 1987 a staff meeting, carefully structured to ensure that every staff member had a voice, resulted in the identification of 22 concerns, which were listed in priority order. Major concerns that Steve had were echoed by the staff. Neither Steve nor I felt that the priorities could be tackled in the order in which they appeared since many had implications for established organizational structures and traditions. However, we did feel that we should respond to the greatest concern of the staff – their own morale. We headed for our second false start!

Our intention was to give ourselves, as a staff group, the opportunity to analyse the reasons for low morale and to suggest ways in which we could work together to raise it. During a meeting we worked individually to make a picture that expressed our feelings about the school. We shared these in pairs, identifying emerging issues and classifying them as 'satisfiers' or 'dissatisfiers'. In groups of four, staff discussed these. We ended the meeting by asking for suggestions, in writing, for action to be taken by, on the one hand, all staff and, on the other, senior management. Reactions from some teachers were noticeably hostile. The initial activity in particular was regarded by some as 'time-wasting'. Steve subsequently categorized suggestions made by staff and shared them with me and some senior teachers, yet we avoided re-visiting them with the whole staff. Later I wondered whether, had we shared them more widely, the meeting might have gained credibility. I concluded that we had not done so 'because the whole thing had been so uncomfortable that we couldn't go back to it'. Steve said: 'It all looked too bald . . . when it was in black and white. I felt that I would find it too difficult presenting this to staff in anything other than a way that looked like a bit of an apology and a bit of self-justification.'

My influence on the structure of both meetings had been significant. In several respects Steve had taken my advice and accepted my suggestions. Consequently I felt responsible for what I considered to be the 'unmitigated disaster' of the second meeting. We paused. Christmas came and went. Steve took up the reins again and together we planned the next term's programme.

We had two aims in mind, with which we were both in agreement, although one reflected Steve's thinking and the other mine. The first was that an understanding of pupils' entitlements should determine our aims for the school and our plans for development. The second was to encourage communication and collaboration between staff members. Staff were asked, in year teams, to list what they thought pupils were entitled to during their time at school, then to pick one entitlement and increase their provision for it. They were also asked to consider how they would monitor their effectiveness. Steve saw this as a 'powerful incentive for thinking out what you were going to tackle and why'. In addition to this initiative year teams were asked to ensure that every member undertook at least one of the following activities: an observation within school, a school visit, attendance on an INSET course. Records of these activities were to be kept in a year team file to be shared with the whole staff. Towards the end of that term, year teams were asked to 'develop general principles to guide future discussions'. The intention was that, as staff became involved, during the next stage of development, in discussions about practicalities, these principles would govern their decision-making.

Although attitudes towards these initiatives varied, a number of staff felt they had benefited from the programme. Steve said:

> It had its difficulties but whatever its ins and outs it started a term which was tremendously beneficial . . . . They felt that they were doing something real and valuable. The fact that they were having to write it all down and share it made it more worthwhile.

During this term our partnership settled. We both felt that the staff group, as a whole, was moving forward and that our role was to guide the processes we had set in motion. This period typified Steve's view of school development, expressed some months later:

> It's a bit like navigating a sailing boat. You aim for your next point and then you have to make a bit of a correction because the tide's carried you off course, but you're always heading in the same direction, prepared to make steady adjustments for course and, perhaps most important, keeping people happy and going the whole while, as it happens.

During the third term staff were organized by Steve into four curriculum groups. Their task was to draw on all they had learned during the previous term in order to make recommendations for the following academic year. During this period Steve and I emphasized the importance of making connections between what had been and what would be, between our deliberations thus far and the decisions to be made about the organization of the school. Such links, we hoped, would provide staff with a combined sense of purpose and continuity. We hoped for some creative thinking during these discussions. However, Steve was conscious of a feeling of disappointment after the early curriculum group meetings, partly because he felt that individual interests had been too much to the fore and partly because he had some preconceived ideas about possible outcomes. Only two meetings of the curriculum groups had taken place before I left the school to take up a new appointment and my partnership with Steve came to an end.

Although there were other tangible outcomes of the programme of school development, such as the more flexible timetable arrangements agreed for the following academic year, I believe the most significant and deeply rooted effect was on the relationships, in particular the role relations, among the staff. These became less authoritarian and more informal. Whereas Selwyn Wyatt had been, as one teacher said, 'outspoken in pointing out that the school could not be a democracy', Steve felt himself unable to be 'prescriptive' and I felt that I was not there 'to impose my own educational philosophy on the school, but to enable things to take place'. This difference in attitude, demonstrated both by our behaviour as people with people and by the strategies we used to bring about school development, served to alter the relationships that had traditionally existed between the senior management (that is, the head and deputy) and the rest of the staff. No longer did the head, aided by the deputy, act as decision-maker and director while staff did as instructed. Rather some staff perceived us as operating from a central, rather than a top-down, position to inspire, encourage and facilitate their increasing collaboration and involvement in school-wide decision-making. Relationships between staff members were also changed by the efforts we made to ensure that every teacher had a voice. Those who had been used to influencing decision-making by private negotiation with the headteacher had now to exercise their personal influence, not with respect to the head alone, but through group processes designed to encourage maximum participation. The importance of the traditional hierarchical structure diminished and the roles of those with posts of responsibility were subtly altered. All staff members had increased power to influence events but formal status came to mean less.

Two main changes, then, resulted from our partnership. One was the relationships between staff and pupils, the other the nature of the role relations between staff members. The first resulted from our behaviour with the pupils and our failure to fulfil the expectations of our colleagues that we would impose authoritarian forms of discipline, and the second from the procedures we used to encourage discussion about and involvement in the process of school development. Both reflected beliefs Steve and I shared about the attitudes and responsibilities of teachers and pupils. I think it probable that, in relation to these beliefs, I learned a good deal about individual responsibility from Steve and he learned about collaboration from me. It is certain that the ways in which we each behaved, founded on the beliefs and values we shared, influenced the process and progress of development at St Thomas.

On reflection it seems that there were two reasons why Steve and I were able to work together and to enable the process of change to take place. One was to do with accord and the other with challenge. There were three substantial areas of agreement between us: we shared a similar approach to teacher–pupil relationships and discipline; we were both committed to the idea of development; we shared a belief in the importance of involving all staff in the process of development and consequently a commitment to seeking strategies that would help to bring this about. These areas of agreement related to means rather than ends. I believe that we differed as to desirable ends, that is in our views of what ought to characterize the learning environment in schools. 'Although Steve and I are similar people and have a similar respect for children the sorts of schools we would come out with would be different. His would be more formal and more structured than mine' (Penny). Such differences might have had greater significance had my appointment been permanent. As it was I believed my role was one of helping with processes, not determining outcomes. Consequently, although it was critical that Steve and I should agree on means, we were able to differ amicably about ends, a luxury not many head–deputy partnerships can afford.

The challenge arose partly from our different professional backgrounds and partly from the task we undertook together. Whereas Steve brought a knowledge of the school to our planning, I brought a knowledge of theory. He gave me the opportunity to put theory into practice and I was able to use theory to challenge his thinking.

> *Steve*: We had a year of working things through in a situation where we could argue and talk things out and where you were able to feel that you were going to make me justify what I was doing rather than just accepting it. I thought that was very good. Certainly good for me from the point of view of having to think more about why I wanted things to be a particular way or what I didn't really want and was only trying to perpetuate because it had always been like that and I was scared to do anything about it.

This challenge made the programme of school development a learning experience for us both, though Steve is more easily able to identify what was of most significance in his learning than I am in mine. He found that, first, his view of the process changed:

> One of the things that I learned is that you really have got to step out into the dark almost, that you have to be sufficiently adventurous, that you've got to take chances and take risks. That's something you often said and it was a new one to me because in the past my ideas of how you managed things was that you worked from a basis of near certainty.

Secondly, his view of his own role in the process changed:

> What I see my role as now is helping to identify broad objectives, sometimes actually doing the identifying but often taking a chairing role in discussing what broad objectives should be, being sensitive to what are the most likely mechanisms for achieving those objectives and trying to enable that process to take place . . . . I think my role is governed by the realization that I can't be the one that determines the exact end point, but I can say that the direction is near enough right.

I find it harder to identify the significant aspects of my own learning because my experience at St Thomas was accompanied by attendance on the MA course and bounded before and after by periods of research on associated themes. My partnership with Steve and our efforts to lead the process of school development were part of a learning experience that extended beyond that particular school and time. Its importance to me was that it provided the opportunity to link theory and practice and to reflect on both. Each of us certainly learned, and learned together, that school development is not a simple matter of planning the steps to achieve pre-determined ends. Rather, to quote from C. S. Lewis (1968: 62) – albeit in a context far removed from school development: 'It seems there are no paths. The going itself is the path.'

A few general conclusions about working and learning together may be reached from a consideration of our story. First, it seems likely that some significant agreement on both beliefs and the interpretation of beliefs in action are necessary for effective collaboration. Secondly, when colleagues share the same beliefs and obviously act in similar ways it may not be necessary further to discuss aims and objectives, either formally or informally, in order to work together towards the same ends. Thirdly, working together provides opportunities for learning, both from and with one another. Finally, difference may be as important to the process of collaboration as similarity. It was, after all, in the tension between significant areas of accord and the challenges arising from our different ways of thinking that Steve and I worked productively together. I shall always be grateful that our partnership was characterized by both.

5

In search of authenticity: learning to be a headteacher

Sheena Ball

I was appointed headteacher of a group 4 junior school in February 1985. At that time we were sharing the building of another school while awaiting the move into a new building constructed on the site of the old, demolished one. The school community had been functioning at a distance of approximately one and a half miles from its catchment area since May 1983. My perception of my main responsibilities as the new headteacher were to re-establish the school in its own locality and community and to change the curriculum of the school in order to improve the quality of education experienced by the children.

This chapter seeks to outline the development of my thinking and consequent action as I grappled with the nature of the role of headteacher. I was, and still am, indebted in my learning to the members of the school community and to colleagues who shared their understandings with me. We discussed, shared and researched together so that subsequent changes would maximize the educational experience of the children for whom we were responsible.

I had, and still have, a vision of education born out of personal experience, debate with educationalists and reading, but in 1985 I was a teacher, not a headteacher. My attention was focused single-mindedly on enriching children's learning. The headteacher's responsibility towards teachers and other adults within the school community was a dimly understood perception. Organizational matters of space were a priority consideration because the new school is of an 'open style', and so I prepared for the challenge of changing the curriculum and styles of organization, to be ready for moving into the new school in February 1986. I embarked on the adventure with the energy of relative youth (33 years) and inexperience, but I was ill-prepared. I had been deputy headteacher of the school for two years and had applied for the post of headteacher only because I felt it was expected of me. The desire to become the headteacher came during the two days of interview. I had been on no management courses, had had no real debate with the previous headteacher and had a naive view of teacher education. I was an inexperienced visionary with a message. The message was simplified and codified for children into *do, discuss, communicate* and *display*, but developing the process with adults proved far more difficult.

I had developed my educational theory during a year's secondment at the Cambridge Institute of Education (1978–9). It is my belief that theory and practice develop in interaction, i.e. that theory becomes embedded in practice and that practice provides the illumination, challenge, tentative justification, falsification and possible transformation of theory. It is a dynamic dialectic of organic development. At that stage in my professional quest for authenticity, however, there was no awareness of this, only a vague dissatisfaction with teaching and learning as I had experienced them thus far. I was offered an 'educative' experience through my own learning and given the space to read, think, debate and theorize. Particular questions are firmly fixed in my memory as initiating episodes of change, such as 'Are you an existentialist?' At that stage I did not know the meaning of the word. The question niggled and so I began to read philosophy. 'Don't you think you can learn from asking and discussing, instead of always reading and thinking?' This was a 'revolutionary' question. Learning for me, I realized, was private and internalized. Schooling was about reception and testing of that reception.

Gradually I constructed a theory of education that I would endeavour to translate into practice on my return to school. It is based on a particular epistemology: that knowledge is not truth. Knowledge is a social construction and has no reality outside of those who know and develop it. It can be regarded as the attempts of individuals to explain their environment and experience. It is grounded in experience (Glaser and Strauss 1976). Experience, however, is not sufficient. If sensation is to become perception there must be an active structuring of the mind:

> There is no need to remind the reader that we base our principal objections to empiricism on the considerable contributions made to perceptual processes by the activities of the subject, and on the role played by choice or decision in those activities. The subject does not submit himself to the constraints of the object, but directs his perceptual activities as if he were solving a problem: he explores, first choosing the point of centration, then relates objects to the contexts, transports, anticipates and so on.
>
> (Piaget 1969: 363)

In Popper's (1966) view observation cannot precede theory, and it is only through theoretical structure that we can perceive elements within our experience. If knowledge derived from experience is impossible without theoretical structures, from where does the child acquire structure? Piaget's work (1958, 1972) suggests that children conceptualize as they do because of an inborn human predisposition so to do. Peters (1970: 49), however, suggests that Piaget 'did not speculate as to the extent to which the development of mind is the product of initiation enshrined in a public language'. Vygotsky's work (1978) suggests that knowledge is culturally determined through the acquisition of language.

Knowledge is, therefore, uncertainty. Its communication structures are culturally determined. Its debates are conducted within mutually accepted systems of rationality which are themselves social constructions. The whole, therefore, is open to falsification. That new 'facts' emerge from the use of different scientific traditions, structures or paradigms has been indicated by Kuhn (1970). A society's knowledge can be extended, reformed and, occasionally, transformed in a creative process whereby individuals move from the accepted and attempt new explanations. The latter, however, is rare as individuals' learning is enculturalized and bounded by the degree to which they have access to the full range of human experience and knowledge debates.

Education is, in consequence, a highly problematical, dynamic process of communication based on first-hand experience and theoretical structure. There is no end-state, either for the process itself or for individuals involved in the process. All individuals engaged in the process must be cognitively active, checking content and theoretical structures against both experience and the 'knowledge' of other individuals involved in the process. All persons, children or adults, should be confident communicators able to share their own understandings, at whatever conceptual level, and to subject their understandings to both internal critical review and the critical questioning of others. Everyone's construal is worthy of respect as all is uncertainty. An arrogant person cannot be an educated person. All educators, at whatever age or level in the system, are by definition both teachers and learners. Education and schooling are not necessarily the same. In fact educative schooling may be a rare and precious reality which easily mutates into an illusory, distorted shadow of itself.

I believed that these new (to me) insights would enable me to transform my classroom practice. I returned to school a debater, no longer shy of the 'expert', and willing to learn. But I had read nothing of the difficulties of initiating and sustaining educational change (Dalin 1978; Fullan 1982), had no understanding of the political nature of schooling and was ill-prepared for challenge and hostility. Fortunately my headteacher was supportive of my efforts as a result of the influence of a newly appointed primary adviser. He, too, had a vision.

The primary adviser had brought together a group of teachers concerned to develop work based on a first-hand experience and I was fortunate to be invited to join the group. The group met fortnightly for two hours from 1978 until 1983. The first hour of each session was given to experiencing first-hand the practical activities in which we were engaging our children. This situation was a necessary nightmare for me as my life experience has made me extremely anxious about engaging in practical work in the company of others. Failure is public and obvious, not private and between the covers of an exercise book. It was necessary, however, 'to get on the inside' of the activities and enjoy success. The second hour was given to relaxed, but increasingly incisive, debate about our shared educational experience and how it was affecting our work with children. I enjoyed the second hour enormously as I was increasingly becoming more skilled at debate, but the whole was an 'educative' experience that gave me the necessary support and challenge to embed conviction and commitment (Polyani 1962) into practice. So I began to become an educator and not simply a teacher.

I was becoming self-reflective (Schon 1983) and beginning the process of becoming a researcher (Rudduck and Hopkins 1985; Elliott 1987). I joined another group formed to work through the Open University's 'Curriculum in Action' material. Some simple, yet potentially complex, questions of evaluation focused my attention on substantiating theory within what the children and I were doing:

1 What did the children do?
2 What were they learning?
3 How worthwhile was it?
4 What did I, the teacher do?
5 What did I learn?
6 What do I intend to do now?

Writing focused my attention on emerging patterns that otherwise might have remained unperceived through the flux of time. Presenting material to critical, yet supporting, colleagues clarified thought. I had not yet heard of action research (Elliott 1981; Whitehead and Foster 1984; Carr and Kemmis 1986; McNiff 1988) but I valued this experience and carried on the self-evaluative approach when the group eventually ceased to meet in 1984. All these experiences enabled me to develop professionally and in confidence and so I entered headship with a sense that there was much to be done, but that it could be done.

By autumn 1986 I was in despair. The school was settled in its new building. We had been entered for, and subsequently received, the Society of Education Officers' Curriculum Award. The local community was once again involved with us. The quality of the children's work in terms of product and presentation had improved, but I had ceased to be an educator. The demands of my new role, as I perceived it, were inconsistent with my substantial self (Nias 1987, 1989). I longed to return to the classroom. I felt incapable of meeting the challenge. The primary adviser suggested I went on a term's fellowship at the West Glamorgan Institute of Education. The subject for consideration was 'Teacher Self-evaluation and Appraisal', but it could have been anything. I shall never forget the sense of release and escape as I left the school building on the last day of term – joy only slightly tinged with the regret that I would eventually have to return.

The essential problem for me was how to improve the quality of children's learning given that it was the teachers who were entrusted with the children's classroom learning. I felt extremely accountable, and therefore vulnerable, yet powerless to effect real change. Every member of staff was working to the best of his or her understanding, yet they also knew that my expectations differed from theirs. I could not communicate my own construal of learning and was in consequence demoralized.

I decided to develop my learning through three strategies. First, I visited 14 schools and interviewed every headteacher and 58 teachers. The schools were chosen because they met some or all of the following criteria: they were well regarded by advisers; they had favourable HMI inspection reports; or they had headteachers who were open and friendly at a personal level. I needed to learn and was not interested in being judgemental or highly critical. The aim of the visits was to find out how headteachers attempted to improve the quality of children's learning. I also wished to find out how and why teachers initiated change and how they regarded the authority dimension of the headteacher's role. Secondly, I decided to deduce from reading, reflecting and discussion what I believe to be the role of the headteacher-educator. Thirdly, I felt an obligation to the title of the fellowship and so decided to try out some of the techniques of teacher self-evaluation with the staff and to monitor the results. So much for sensitivity and wisdom.

Any insights gained from my discussions with teachers and headteachers are constrained by numerous factors. I was involved in a learning process and my perceptions were limited by my own understanding and embryonic research skills. Some headteachers refused access to teachers whom they considered reluctant to change; others selected teachers, hoping that they would learn something specific from their responses. However, I was not in a position to help them in this way as it would have broken confidentiality. Some left the decisions on whether they become involved to the teachers themselves and others told the whole staff that they had to be interviewed. By this stage I was so grateful that anyone would speak to me that I interviewed all who presented themselves and simply asked why they had 'volunteered'. However, it was difficult to assess in any way the 'truthfulness' of what people said. Some interview data may be suspect because of personality conflicts, prejudice or fear of reprisal. Early on I realized that this was an issue, as a result of remarks such as 'I've told you things we're supposed to. Now do you really want to hear what it's really like?'

The interview data indicate that in 1987 education in the majority of the visited schools was characterized by a greater or lesser degree of uncertainty and confusion. Few teachers seemed able to articulate the reasons why they were engaged in practices, some of which they did not believe in. For example:

I wish the experts would start agreeing so I could tell the teachers. (headteacher)

I've never really questioned this. You do what you should. [Interpreted later as what authority tells you.] (teacher)

Do you think I'm right? (teacher)

I don't think why; I have faith and hope. (teacher)

It must be right. The adviser likes it. (teacher)

Change is coming from everywhere. It's all change. How can we know what to change? When will I find time to change everything? Can you ever change anything? (headteacher)

Uncertainty is an integral factor within education and can lead to creative episodes of learning. Much of the uncertainty I encountered, however, was characterized by anxiety, which can negate the learning process (Holt 1969). The roots of the uncertainty are found in the nature of modern British society. Many ideologies coexist with varying degrees of consensus and conflict. The materialistic forces of the market place seem to dominate, but are not universally adhered to, as religious, humanistic and alternative political ideologies continue to exist. Schools are microcosms of wider society and teachers will also adhere, whether consciously or unconsciously, to varying belief and value systems.

We are all products of, and contributors to, society. From our earliest days the innate self is locked in interaction within the conforming processes of socialization. A degree of creativity and autonomy is possible, but the social constructions of language and rationality are powerful forces for consensus. However, schools are often conforming institutions. They exist to 'educate' the young, i.e. to involve them in debate and communication based on experience, but many of their activities are antithetical to debate. The practices of schooling, generally, appear to pass down from generation to generation, encouraged by a widespread deference to 'authority'.

I don't say much in staff meetings. I let the older ones get on with it. I'm worried about saying the wrong thing. (probationary teacher)

You learn from senior teachers you respect. (teacher)

The head's decision is what it has to be at the end of the day. (teacher)

In a stable society of uniform culture the transmission of culture would seem non-problematic, but in a pluralist society the conformity is surprising.

The roots of conformity to 'traditional' schooling practices probably lie in the schooling experienced by teachers themselves. The vast majority of teachers seem to have been schooled within the didactic tradition. If they have experienced nothing else, then they 'know' nothing else. Indeed, teachers who claimed to have made changes in their teaching style referred to educative experiences within their own development:

> It was the doing and discussing with other teachers. (teacher)

> You learnt skills by doing. The discussions and sharing ideas at the exhibition at the end helped me most. (teacher)

> Workshop sessions and discussion are better. You are involved and you feel what to do with the children. (teacher)

Other teachers claimed that they had changed, but they appeared to be referring to organizational matters and the presentation of end-products rather than the educational process itself. It is fairly easy to make a class-room appear 'informal' in terms of high quality display, arrangement of furniture and differentiation of tasks, while at the same time maintaining a highly didactic mode of interaction between teacher and child. The end result of the curriculum movements of the 1960s and 1970s appeared to be a moving of the didactic voice of the teacher on to the didactic voice of the worksheet, in the name of 'individuality', 'integration' and 'informality'. High cognition has been sacrificed on the altar of the duplicating machine. Tired teacher technicians pass on to children the skills of coping with repetition, boredom and 'waiting your turn'. There has been no conscious decision to deceive. Teachers, like everyone else, can only assimilate new ideas to their cognition, which is bounded by their own experience.

Responsibility for educational decision-making rested with 'authority', leading upwards through a hierarchical chain to 'them'. Headteachers were expected to be in authority. However, a paradox existed. Some teachers appeared to want to be told, yet resented being told. They depended on the authority of others but resented authoritarianism. As a result, authority was sometimes subverted rather than engaged in critical debate:

> We asked her three times to explain the form designed to enable teachers to self-evaluate as we did not understand it. In the end she said 'Fill it in.' So we waited until she was at a meeting, took hers off her desk and copied it on to ours. We changed a few ticks so she wouldn't notice. It kept her happy, but it didn't mean a thing. (teacher)

> You know what 'good primary practice' is supposed to look like. So when we're having visitors we get out the weaving, the computer, the paints and the pastels. It's not like that normally. The children may have done the work, but who knows except us that it might have been three years ago. (teacher)

No wonder I could not communicate with my own staff. I was proposing the absence of authoritarianism from the perspective of a role perceived by the persons I was attempting to communicate with as being highly authoritarian. There was little in their experience to suggest that schooling could be otherwise. I began to see that the 'problem' lay in my own lack of perception. It seemed that the key to curriculum development is teacher education. If teachers are to involve children in educational processes then they, too, must experience the empowerment that can come from critical debate and communication grounded in experience.

As a result of this insight I attempted to involve the teachers in self-evaluation of their own classroom practice. Debate would be based on recent experience. First, I prepared a diary form and its accompanying reflection sheet, to be worked on by the next meeting (Figures 5.1 and 5.2). Participation was voluntary, but everyone became involved from the outset. The discussion sheet (Figure 5.3) was presented at the subsequent meeting. We began the next meeting in two small discussion groups. I excluded myself from both. We then came together as one group chaired by me. I subsequently wrote up the minutes and circulated them to all group members. I left an observation schedule and second reflection sheet to be considered by the next meeting (Figures 5.4 and 5.5). My personal self-evaluation of the first meeting reads, 'You are not very good at asking ope-ended questions and must learn when to keep quiet when chairing discussions.'

The next meeting took a similar format (Figure 5.6). I felt that I handled the whole-group meeting more successfully as I was less anxious. Some teachers began to share insights gained from observing the children and the implications for their own practice. One teacher indicated that self-evaluation increased guilt feelings. This was something I was acutely aware of in my own experience and so I explained my view of educational theory as it applies to our learning, i.e. that we should adopt a research model in our approach to our work. Apparent failure need not induce guilt as we have learnt something. There was tentative agreement.

By now I had learnt that teachers are not always aware of their own values and that they cannot truly self-evaluate until their philosophy is made explicit to themselves. I was still not secure enough to risk the exposure of a value system contradicting my own so I gave the teachers an extract from *About our Schools* by Sir Alec Clegg (1980) and a third reflection sheet (Figures 5.7 and 5.8).

The subsequent discussion, which was whole-group, proved to be highly profitable. Considerable discussion took place about the initial fear that probationary teaches have of losing control. Control is sometimes established by fear, which reflects the teacher's own fear. Learning then takes a poor second place and you can become stuck in the mould. Discussions also centred on what we meant by quality work and the principles we wished

Figure 5.1 The diary form

Suggested Diary Form (Please feel free to alter) Write down the two most significant events in each session:
Break
Lunch
Break
This sheet is the personal property of the writer and NO ONE has right of access.

Figure 5.2 The reflection sheet accompanying the diary form

Reflection Sheet

Please bring the diary sheets and this sheet to the next meeting but I will not read them unless you wish me to. Neither should you feel obliged to discuss the contents.

1 Why did you choose these events and not any other?

2 What does this choice of events indicate to you about what *you* really believe is important in how children learn?

3 Does any of your data indicate to you that you should make changes to maximize learning? What and how?

4 Make the change(s) (one at a time?) and monitor what happens. If you wish, ask for advice and/or support in making the change, but that is not essential. You are a responsible professional. (Note: Other professional views can be helpful.)

5 Has this exercise helped you in thinking about how people learn? If yes, what and how?

6 Is the exercise worth repeating? Why?

Figure 5.3 The first discussion sheet

Please discuss
Diaries:

1 Has this exercise helped you in thinking about what the children do in your
   classroom?

2 Has this exercise helped you in thinking about what you do in the classroom?

3 Is it worth repeating?

4 Why?

5 Would you alter the exercise in any way?

6 Is there any help you need in your classroom teaching, now?

Figure 5.4 The observation schedule

Observation

Find 10 minutes when you can observe rather than interact with the children. Choose one child.

1 What is the child supposed to be doing?

2 Record on the sheet what he/she is really doing.

Minute	Observation	Any relevant comments

Study the data:

1 Should *you* have done something differently?

2 What change(s) can you make?

Figure 5.5 The reflection sheet accompanying the observation schedule

---

Reflection Sheet 2

A If you did not fill in the observation sheet was it because:

    1 You viewed it as a kind of a test and were afraid you'd complete it
      incorrectly? (If so I apologize that I have been doing my job badly.) Any
      implications for the learning of the children in your class?

    2 You couldn't find the time? Any implications for classroom management?

B If you did fill it in:

    1 Was it a useful means of gathering information about the learning in your
      classroom?

    2 Any difficulties encountered?

If you wish, yourself, to carry on with the idea please feel free to modify it to
suit your own needs.

Please bring the observation sheet and this sheet to the next meeting, but no one
will read them and you should not feel obliged to discuss the contents.

Figure 5.6   The second discussion sheet

Discussion Sheet

1 Has this exercise been of any value?

2 If, yes, why?

3 If no, why not?

4 Were you surprised at any of the information revealed?

5 Are there any personal insights resulting from the exercise that you are prepared to share?

6 It has been suggested that this kind of observation sheet may be valuable as
part of a record-keeping system. What do you think?

If yes, is it possible time-wise? For example, at the rate of one per child per
term it would mean three a week.

If not, why?

Figure 5.7 Extract from *About Our Schools* given to teachers

Extract from About Our Schools by Sir Alec Clegg

There are, I believe, certain qualities which exist in any first-class teacher, whether he teaches formally or informally. The following are some of these qualities:

He believes that love is a better spur to learning than fear.

He agrees with Montaigne that more often than not 'savoir par coeur n'est pas savoir'.

He believes that the sort of person a child becomes is often more important than what he knows.

He is hesitant about accepting a syllabus of learning prescribed by an examination or devised by a person who has no knowledge of the background of the children in his class.

He tries to ensure that every child has an experience of success and he acclaims this success and tries to build on it.

He knows the lamentable effect on children of incessant failure.

He knows the limitations of trying to measure what a child has learned and he uses measurement with wise discrimination.

He knows and acts on the fact that delight in the performance of a skill is essential to the real mastery of it.

He gives responsibility not only to children who can discharge it but also to children whose development needs this experience.

He knows how to encourage older children to help the young and the strong to help the frail.

He uses knowledge as material for the mind to work on, and not as a lump of matter to be forced into a container.

He understands the very full part that parents can and should play in education and he maintains a fruitful contact with them and often uses them wisely in school.

He knows that there are times when he will be more effective if he works with a group of colleagues than if he works singly.

He knows it is part of his job to cultivate initiative, sensitivity and confidence as well as to impart facts.

He knows what he means by good behaviour and he knows how to secure it from his children.

He knows that knowledge is doubling every decade or so and that the bit of it that he uses to stimulate his children today may be very different from the bits he used five years ago, and the bit he will use five years hence.

He knows that a number of his pupils will follow the educational route which he followed but he is particularly careful to try and understand the hopes and fears, the loves and hates, the enthusiasms and antipathies of youngsters who are far less well endowed than he himself and than the majority of his class.

He knows also that a number of his pupils will have come from homes with very little support and resource and that somehow this will have to be made up to them.

He knows that each child is subject to different pressures and influences and he tries to harness the better pressures to his use and to counteract the bad ones.

In particular he knows of the many ways in which a child can be handicapped and disadvantaged and he does all in his power to help these special cases.

Figure 5.8   The reflection sheet accompanying the extract

Reflection Sheet 3

Please read carefully this extract from *About Our Schools* by Sir Alec Clegg. Read it *before* considering the following:

1 Which value statement has struck you most forcibly?

2 Why?

3 Do you agree with it?

4 Why, or why not?

5 If you agree: does your classroom really match up to it? (Honest.) Think and look tomorrow. If you wish to write a response please do so. You can share it if you wish or keep it personal.

6 If you don't agree with that particular value statement choose one that you do and work on number 5.

7 Please write a *short* response to the extract. (Please take note, *short*.) You may be asked to share the response with the whole group.

---

to establish when displaying children's work. Every teacher found his or her voice and some began to reveal their own values and difficulties. We appeared to trust each other. Honesty and vulnerability began to become accepted.

The next stage of significant development for some members of the school staff has been an involvement in action research. Self-evaluation becomes action research when teachers' individualized reflections on the consequences of their action(s) become systematized in a report open to public critique. Publication 'opens work to criticism and consequently to refinement, and it also disseminates the fruits of research and hence makes possible the cumulation of knowledge' (Rudduck and Hopkins 1985: 17–18).

Unfortunately a tension exists between our commitment to action research and the demands of the 1988 Education Act, with particular reference to the National Curriculum. We work at a point of tension and incompatibility between contradictory epistemologies. The didactic voice of authority is legalized and in print. Heightened debate can be challenging and creative, but all debate can be, and now often is, foreclosed by 'it is written'. This is a tension which has to be resolved within each educator. I cannot speculate on the future, but I have been fortunate to have been engaged in an educational process. From now on, I cannot be satisfied with less. For one thing, our children are entitled to an education and teachers deserve professional respect. For another, teachers who have experienced professional development and have developed interaction with children within educational processes cannot forget their experiences.

The improving of our schools as educational centres concerned with maximizing and extending children's potential is a demanding task. My experience leads me to believe that reflective educators, rather than legislation, are most likely to enhance children's learning. Such professionals, however, benefit from working within supportive staff groups or linked to groups of like-minded colleagues. I hold such colleagues to be of inestimable value in my own development.

6

Working together: being a member of a teachers' group

Mary Heath

In September 1988 I became a member of a group of teachers who were interested in children's writing development and the relationship of talking to writing. My membership of that group and the friendship of the women who made up the group were to extend my thinking about the ways in which we as teachers can work and learn together. But the story of my learning did not start all at once at that point. Rather, it was a place in the narrative to which I could point and say: 'Here the experience became qualitatively different.' We all had a shared background of involvement in the National Writing Project, through which some of us first met. We were already part of a larger group of primary and middle school teachers – the National Writing Project in Bedfordshire – who had worked together for a period of two years. Therefore this part of the story has to be told first, before the implications of the new group can be considered.

The National Writing Project in Bedfordshire

The National Writing Project was set up by the Schools Curriculum Development Committee (SCDC) in 1985. Bedfordshire was invited to work with the project for two years from September 1986 and I became the coordinator of the county-wide initiative. We were to look at ways in which the microcomputer, particularly the word processor, might help in the development of children's writing. During these two years we met together after school every fortnight, worked in one another's classrooms, shared writing days, planned workshops together and published and read each other's writing. The framework of the National Writing Project, including the support that could be given to teachers from myself as the coordinator, encouraged everyone to talk about their ideas and to share them with a wider audience, through writing for local and national journals. Other teachers could then try out the ideas, if they seemed appropriate to them at that time. The National Writing Project became visible and concrete through the ordinary, quiet and thoughtful work of the individuals in the local groups. It became excitingly clear that there was a consensus of opinion about children, writing and learning developing from the Project's classroom work. This gave us all a sense of confidence, community and strength because we were in control, both personally and as a group, of the writing curriculum we were developing and the school context within which it was finding a place. We came to realize how far these elements were necessary, valuable and integral to our own learning. So we looked for further ways that we could talk with our colleagues about our teaching practice, the reasons which lay behind it and the excitement we found within it.

There is no doubt that teachers were empowered to make changes to aspects of their classroom practice because the Project supported them in three ways:

1 The teachers knew that their work and experimentation with new ideas was not only valued and respected by the county and by the national team, but that it was expected as part of the commitment to the Project itself.
2 As the coordinator of the local project, I had time to work alongside the teachers in their classrooms as they tried out their ideas, and I was in a unique position to carry ideas and enthusiasms around the county from one teacher to another.
3 There was a small amount of money within the Project which was used to release teachers from their classroom responsibilities so that we could all meet during the day.

Furthermore, the curriculum that the children experienced was enhanced, as the teachers asked the questions they thought were important about how the children learned to write and as they sought answers both from their own resources and from those of the group of teachers who were called the National Writing Project. We were looking at ourselves as learners as well as at the children. We were working together as a community whose endeavour was to work towards a better understanding of the concept of education. It was challenging and creative work. The way we were able to share ideas within the group was enabling us to talk about ourselves as learners and to understand that we had some control over the conditions and context of our own learning. A group of us within the Bedfordshire Project wanted this way of working together to continue. This was the background to the formation of the curriculum development group that was to look at the value of talk in the writing process.

The setting up of the new group

We were a group of eight women teachers. We were primary teachers, except for one English lecturer from the local college of higher education. We had worked together and talked together and we wanted to continue doing so in an informal but productive way. We had already learned from our involvement in the Writing Project that changes in both perceptions and practice take time to develop and to be implemented. They are liable to cause unease and concern and those who are in the middle of the process of change need support, encouragement and the presence of others who are interested and understand the need to talk because they are themselves experiencing change. We turned to each other as a group of familiar people. We had become able to work together. We had all enjoyed the shared classroom work and the sharing of ideas. We felt that we were at an important stage in the development of our thinking about how children learned to write and the ways in which we could create a better context for that learning to take place. We felt sure that we would benefit from continuing to work together. We were proud to have been part of the National Writing Project and now as a group of women who had 'travelled together through writing, and found it beneficial', as one of our group put it, we had become a group of friends. This helped us to work for further change because we were more honest with each other about classroom practice.

I was coming to the end of a two-year part-time research degree and, because I was returning to my work as a special education support teacher before becoming a deputy head in a first school, I was planning to do my dissertation in an area that would allow me to bridge the gap between that and my work as the coordinator of the Writing Project. By this time the group had decided to continue working together and I thought that this transition time from one group to another would be worth documenting. Each member agreed that I might tape record the meetings. I did this and during the October half-term I transcribed four meetings: two early meetings in May and June, which were the planning meetings for the September start of the new group, and two in the autumn term. I sent a copy of these to each member of the group. Then I began to listen closely to the recordings. We had talked about the Writing Project, about the name for the new group, about the meeting place, about Sue's laptop computer – conversation between a group of people who were preparing for a new initiative and a new stage in their professional lives. But now the words of that conversation were also held steady on the pages of my transcription and I was able to query interpretation, hear that each teacher had a different talking style, how sometimes we each trod on the important pauses and filled the gaps without leaving room for anyone else. I scrutinized the text, searching for reasons and asking questions to which I wanted an answer. In November I was able to talk privately to four of the seven women in the scant time that we had available. I met them in their place of work and suddenly the talking became an interview. I thought then, as now, that the semi-formality of the occasion indicated to the women a seriousness on my part, that I did indeed want to hear what they had to say, and this encouraged them to speak openly. It was during this time that I learned about their fears for the new group, about their feelings of pleasure that they had been involved in the Writing Project and about the way in which that had helped them to make changes in their classrooms. My perceptions of similar experiences were not the same as theirs. Yet although at times I became defensive and at times bemused by the unexpectedness of the replies, I learned to listen to their answers and consider them in the light of my understanding. It was hard, thought-provoking work.

I transcribed each taped interview and sent it to the interviewee with a synopsis at the bottom, summarizing what I thought we had talked about. At this point I received an enthusiastic response, a flurry of letters, telephone calls and further conversations. I then wrote a first draft of my study and circulated it to all the group. This was accepted by the group with minor amendments as the basis for the next stage of my work. They wished to keep their own names in the text and they agreed that the writing would be available for other colleagues to read. Fortunately the word processor facilitated the writing up of this research, which was responsive to the views of the group and depended upon their cooperation in it. It was certainly exciting for me and, as far as I can measure from their encouraging responses, exciting for my colleagues too. Vivian wrote to me after I had sent her a draft copy of the study, saying:

> I had the weird feeling that I was reading my own 'life story' in a way.
> I don't know what I expected but I do find it interesting and, yes, I
> do feel involved – and privileged to have been involved in the Writing
> Project, when I read what you had written – more so than before I
> read it. I suppose reading it has raised my level of consciousness.

In other words we were now closely involved in the work that we were encouraging the children to do: learning through talking and writing. Moreover, not only were the two forms of communication needed to develop the ways in which we were able to communicate with each other, but we were using many, varied aspects of talking and writing as we worked towards mutual understandings and an agreed public presentation of our thinking.

We had met in September 1988 with an equal responsibility for the new group's survival. We set our own agenda and determined our own ways of working, and our own ways of reporting that work. We all had to travel to reach a central meeting place. With the impact of the new legislation for the implementation of the National Curriculum we also had an increased workload at school and many more school-based demands on our time. At each meeting we needed time to express our feelings about

the national changes that were taking place. The talking and joint negotiation of our understanding of possible outcomes helped us to come to
terms with our own concerns. Such talking slowed down the pace of
change and allowed us time to see what alternatives we had in relation to
our own practice.

Gradually the group itself came under threat, however. From the beginning the other members of the group had expressed their fears about its
viability. I had been surprised by their concerns; I had had no doubts that
this was to be the beginning of a long-term curriculum development group.
Yet their fears were justified. After only nine months we were searching for
a way to resolve several unexpected dilemmas. Although we found the
group very valuable as a means of working and learning together for change,
we now faced new conditions. Over the months it became clear that the
Writing Project had allowed us the time and the space to work together and
this could not now be recreated. There was no money for the supply cover
which would have freed us to go into each other's classrooms during the
time that the children were there, and we missed the stimulus of working
together in classrooms. We needed to talk to each other as friends, yet we
could not meet at any times other than for the work-oriented group meetings
because of pressure from the statutory demands on our time. So we reluctantly decided that we would have to work, for a time, with the people
who were nearest to us geographically. The group disbanded into twos and
threes.

A reflection on the group

As part of the group we each gained a deeper level of understanding about
the ways in which we were responding to one another. We all made space
for everyone to speak and to be heard. We learned to listen closely to each
other and to help each other understand our experiences. We learned to
trust our intuitions and our judgements. We had not planned that our group
would have only women members, but this was important. It meant that
our learning was grounded in three complementary factors: our friendships
as women, our understanding of each other's perspective and a deeper
understanding of our own.

Each of these itself grew from active group membership. Each member
of the group accepted a responsibility to the others to be an involved,
reflective participant. This had several consequences. First, the group
welcomed differences and discussions for the varying and interesting views
they gave on each issue. Secondly, we learned to clarify our own thinking,
as thoughts became tentative words and thus accessible to the scrutiny of
the speaker, as well as to the listeners, and as we questioned each other's
use of words. We saw each other as rational people and we wanted to

explore the other person's meanings as well as our own. Thirdly, we knew that each of us needed to explore her thinking through the stories we told, that there were times when we needed to be discursive. We were aware that through the talk, which sometimes spiralled round and round, we became clear about the work we wanted to tackle, both collectively and individually. Fourthly, we learned to validate and explain the making of choices, and worked towards a clearer understanding of our roles as people within the social setting called school. Fifthly, we became more aware of what the process of change might mean for the colleagues with whom we worked. Finally, we also became more aware of the opportunities for change in our daily work with the children which lay within our grasp as teachers. Our discussions led us to look more closely at the children as learners because we were more conscious of ourselves as learners. The views we brought to the group came from our teaching practice and we had always intended that our discussions would feed back into our work. Although we were not always sure that they did, talking and listening clarified for us the possibilities that we faced.

I know that my membership of this group of teachers has been an important factor in my personal development. The interaction with these women friends has helped me, perhaps even forced me, to distinguish myself and my ideas from them and their ideas. As I listened to them I was more able to listen to myself. I know that I have reshaped and reinforced my views about schooling through my reflection on the group and on my place in it. Through my work with the group I came to realize that we had to learn to talk openly to each other before we could agree, with a full commitment from everyone, on the direction in which we could travel. I agree with David Marquand that:

> We cannot redefine our common purposes if we cannot have com-
> mon purposes. We cannot educate each other if we have no space in
> which to speak to each other. We cannot learn from each other if we
> will not accept the responsibility for our mistakes.
>
> (Marquand 1988: 231)

This is knowledge that I have worked hard to acquire. It is knowledge about myself and about teaching and learning from which I cannot retreat. It has enabled me to have control over, and an understanding of, the reasons behind my decisions to take action. I become involved in a repositioning, realignment and resorting of my own bases for action. In this way, by talk-ing and learning together, we are changed. I have come to realize that, if we wish to change the experience of schooling for the majority, we have to create a place and a time within education where there can be 'quiet pro-cesses and small circles in which vital and transforming events take place' (Rutledge 1988: 230).

I know that this is long-term thinking. It cannot happen immediately. But it will not happen at all unless it is planned for and every small step is valued and acknowledged. I have learned this from the group of which I was part. As we each work towards creating a community of learners and teachers we need to know that 'Solidarity has to be constructed out of little pieces, rather than found already waiting' (Rorty 1989: 9).

7

Learning to help others

Jay Mawdsley

The page of life that was spread out before me seemed
dull and commonplace, only because I had not fathomed
out its deeper import . . . . The wiser effort would have been
to diffuse thought and imagination through the opaque
substance of today, and thus to make it a bright
transparency . . . to seek resolutely the true and
indestructible value that lay hidden . . . in the incidents and
ordinary characters with which I was now conversant.

(Nathaniel Hawthorn, *The Scarlet Letter*)

On the threshold

'Why leave your own classroom to work in other people's classrooms?' This
question may not always be asked in such a direct manner but it is
nevertheless one that seems to intrigue fellow teachers as they gently probe
for a satisfactory answer. Why leave the vertical career pathway of teacher,
deputy head and headteacher and take a sideways move out of the classroom? Is this an escape route or a search for a new challenge?

The questions I asked of myself are no less perplexing. What are the
challenges and the rewards now that I am no longer directly concerned
with children's learning but trying to work and learn with other teachers? Is
it possible to keep in contact with the reality of classroom life? When I
chose to become an advisory teacher the answers to such questions were
elusive. They carried within them the challenge of the complexity and
ambiguity of the advisory role. In this chapter I shall explore the paradox

of providing teachers with 'advice' and 'support' within the overall context of the National Writing Project. I shall describe my own experience of change, the diffidence of others and the value of the support group.

Know thyself

Taking up an appointment as an advisory teacher placed me immediately in the role of the outsider: fully belonging in neither the classroom nor the advisory service. In many senses I was truly 'semi-detached' (Biott 1991). As a member of this isolated club, or perhaps 'a club of isolates', I was charged with fulfilling the role of offering both curriculum advice and support to teachers. Within the delicate balance of this role lay the challenge of my position.

It seemed axiomatic that, on leaving the full-time position of classroom teacher, I faced a rapidly diminished sense of classroom credibility. The validity of the opinions and suggestions of one who is no longer dealing with the reality of the daily pressures of school is quickly called into question. I was concerned about why and how I offered advice and support for change when I had no confidence that it would be accepted.

As a teacher fresh from the classroom I tried to take confidence from personal experience but to acquire a similar level of confidence in 'teaching' adults takes time. Moreover, as I accumulated experience of an appropriate pedagogy for working with teachers, the relevance of my classroom credibility may have been further called into question. For any learning relationship to flourish there has to be a basis of mutual respect and trust. Without these qualities there can seldom be genuine self-enquiry, and lacking this there is little opportunity for personal growth. My appointment as an advisory teacher probably arose from other people's favourable judgements about my own classroom practice in language teaching. But how many new advisory teachers realize at the outset that this very recognition may present an initial barrier to forming a relationship of mutual respect and trust?

Members of an advisory support team know that, like most teachers, we have had our share of good and bad days in the classroom. Yet our new positions may seem to deny that possibility in the minds of the teachers with whom we are working. Unless we are sensitive to this possible misconception of the advisory teacher as endowed with super-skills, an aura of unachievable standards will cling to the relationship. This may result in advisory teachers being expected to give solutions rather than to forge learning partnerships for developmental change. At the same time, there will be teachers who reject support from those of us who have left the classroom, believing that we have nothing relevant to offer.

How then, as an advisory teacher and project coordinator, could I best establish change-enhancing relationships with other teachers? I was convinced of the need to eschew a pre-packaged, systems model of support. The answer seemed to lie in knowing myself and being prepared to take risks. As Rogers (1983) asserts, the most basic of the essential attitudes to learning is 'realness, or genuineness, or . . . the absence of a front or a facade'.

So it seemed that the first small, but important, step must be taken with caution and a sensitivity about how I might be perceived in schools. At the very least I needed to clarify my own view of the new 'semi-detached role'. It is not, and cannot be, the same as working in a classroom, full-time, five days a week. Nevertheless, in a spirit of genuine collaborative enquiry I hoped for mutual professional learning about the complexity of curriculum development in the classroom.

Setting the agenda

A learning partnership role may not fit with the notions of classroom support that many teachers expect from an advisory teacher. Teachers may hold views of a sharply defined model of curriculum leadership. They may prefer solutions and answers to enquiries and questions. Classroom teachers often regarded the idea of curriculum enquiry with deep suspicion. Self-preservation may alert them to a view of enquiry as additional work in an already over-stretched schedule.

Teachers ask questions – and they hold back too. As an advisory teacher I tried to be conscious of questions that were not articulated directly. Paradoxically, the hidden agenda needs to be kept firmly in view. So it was the reality of the classroom that provided the most appropriate starting point for a curriculum enquiry, and it forced me to acknowledge the unsystematic nature and messiness of change. I became aware of the difficulties of finding an evolving focus for a curriculum enquiry which was clear to both partners and which arose from shared questions and concerns. I also recognized, at the same time, that agendas which are brought to classrooms, rather than arising from them, are likely to hinder genuine learning partnerships.

For this reason, the notion of 'looking anew' was the springboard for coordination of the National Writing Project in Newcastle upon Tyne. At the start of the enquiry into 'Writing in the Early Years', action was deliberately focused on classroom observation. Project teachers shared what they had seen within cluster groups of teachers from different schools.

The choice of schools for the project was based on the premise that, if curriculum change was to lead to enduring development in the LEA, the findings of the teachers needed to be generalized to schools throughout the city. The project was based in 12 schools that were selected to provide a representative cross-section of the varying socioeconomic and demographic catchments in the city. Within the 12 schools, the teachers who joined the project worked with children in the 3–5, 5–7 and 7–9 age groups. By their own admission, however, many of these teachers would not have chosen to opt into the project.

The teachers' initial responses to finding themselves part of the project ranged from feeling 'pleased about the challenge', 'excited but apprehensive', to 'uncertain and apprehensive', 'very much lacking in self-confidence and expertise' and 'totally tricked into it, in total ignorance and very cross'. It was this declared lack of confidence that persuaded us to initiate the exploration of early writing from observation in the classrooms. Starting with, or introducing, theoretical evidence at the wrong time could well have been construed as intimidating. Just as 'beginning writers' are nearly always presented with the mystique of 'end product' writing, which does little to unveil the true nature of composing, so might evidence from research papers be quite as overwhelming for the teacher who is new to curriculum enquiry. I decided that published research should not be allowed to dominate or distort teachers' often fragile confidence as action researchers investigating their own classroom practice for the first time. I introduced articles on writing only when the teachers had evidence of their own against which to evaluate the research findings. Russell (1988: 33) cites teachers' views that support this decision: 'Experience, including one's present teaching practices, shapes the meaning that we read into research, theory, and other sources of recommendations for changes in practice.' Having three age-specific groups meant that each had a separate 'expert' focus for the classroom enquiry. Findings were then shared across the groups, at meetings of the whole project. The classroom-based studies would, I hoped, create an opportunity for teachers to build a collegial context for curriculum development within their cluster groups, an awareness that, in the words of Carl Rogers, 'What is most personal is most general' (Rogers 1961: 26).

Each of the cluster groups worked with a designated cluster leader, for whom the LEA provided a half timetable for work with the writing project. Cluster leaders used most of their time to provide support for teachers within the classroom or to release teachers to work with other project colleagues. The opportunity to work with fellow professionals is a form of INSET that seemed to outweigh by far its costs with the benefits of professional development. Indeed, as coordinator, I found that the sharing of insights into the process of change was invaluable.

Overall, however, the rewards for advisory teaching were elusive and often unexpected. They came from shared insights, from classroom observation and collaboration with colleagues, and from the often casual comments of participating teachers. There were inherent tensions in the job; days when I seemed to have fulfilled nobody's needs; days when I identified with the model of parasitic 'technical bandit' and weeks when I chased time, just keeping the plates spinning in the air.

Offering professional learning support to others had the effect of producing a corresponding growth and development of skills for me. The unique opportunity for personal and professional growth, the breadth of experience and the chance to work with a variety of teachers and children provided an opportunity for opening my eyes afresh. The challenges and rewards were many and varied, both long- and short-term. I had to check my preconceptions about how other people learn and then learn myself how best to develop relationships with fellow learners.

Advisory teaching can be judged according to both short- and long-term objectives using political, economic and pedagogical criteria. Ultimately, as an advisory teacher, I hoped that teachers, and children, would have been empowered for the future, beyond the boundaries of the particular curriculum project. I hoped for a sense of collegiality but realistically I knew that sustained curriculum development only comes about when members of a school continue to share a common concern and show this by raising questions, querying self-practice and evaluating change collaboratively over time.

Discussion about the role of an advisory teacher, or coordinator, makes demands on a vocabulary of ambiguities: words such as tensions, complexity, relationships and paradox become commonplace. They may best be captured by the word 'mystery' and the understanding that as an advisory teacher one joins a group whose members are constantly enquiring, in the knowledge that 'those who are willing to be vulnerable walk among mysteries' (Theodore Roethke 1968), and that mysteries are seldom resolved with neatly labelled solutions. For the future, whether I remain semi-detached, return to the classroom full-time or move out into other spheres of education, the experience of working as an advisory support teacher leaves me vulnerable to the knowledge of how much more there is to know about working and learning together for change.

8

Insight, direction and support: a case study of collaborative enquiry in classroom research

Andy Convery

'Working and learning together for change' might be one description of teachers' everyday professional activity, since they often appear to be engrossed in discussing their classroom experiences. However, mutual development may be not a routine activity, but rather a process that is strongly resisted. In one sense, the notion of teachers working and learning together for change seems to be part of the professional development sessions which now regularly occur in education. In my local experience, training days are an admission that social, political and educational developments, such as the National Curriculum, demand a coherent response from a teaching body. Staff tend to accept the idea that external innovations – new examining bodies, new syllabuses, new technology – will necessitate change, rethinking and reorganization. Their view of change implies the defending and reshaping of existing good teaching practice in response to the initiatives of those outside schools. 'Learning together' is a shared experience because external impositions engender cameraderie between teachers against a common enemy. Change is perceived as an external force, in the face of which groups of teachers openly and enthusiastically work together to adopt and develop practical and strategic responses.

As a teacher I strongly resisted one form of change – that which implied that my existing classroom teaching behaviour was ineffective and therefore needed fundamental alteration. When I investigated my classroom experiences as part of an MA course, my insecurity as a teacher unconsciously drove me to adopt a classroom research plan that avoided self-examination, and validated and affirmed my established style. After eight years of effort and innovation I was unwilling to admit to myself that I was still an inefficient teacher; consequently, I was not prepared seriously to expose my professional self to other colleagues who were apparently satisfied with their classroom competence.

In other words, through my research, I discovered that it was relatively easy to discuss externally administered changes with my colleagues in the staffroom, but it was extremely difficult to investigate my daily classroom practice and open it to the critical examination of my peers, as this would involve making myself personally and professionally vulnerable. In the event, my actual research experience indicated that when others – researchers, students and a colleague – did focus on my classroom experience, they were extremely supportive and helped me to create a more effective and enjoyable classroom learning experience for myself and my students. Initially, I strongly resisted collaborative enquiry. This chapter relates the process of how my reluctance to recognize the need for personal change gradually developed into a series of collaborative activities which helped me understand, and deal with, my problems as a teacher. The account also focuses on the nature of support from a colleague which was necessary to ensure that strategies for change were actually implemented in my classroom.

Researching in isolation

I began my classroom investigations as part of an MA study. I had identified a problem – that when I used television programmes in teaching A-level Communication Studies, the students' reactions were often very limited, and there was no evidence that the programmes were stimulating the response and interest which I had anticipated. Having focused on a problem, my immediate response was to regard it as an external difficulty, shifting my research safely away from my classroom and my teaching. I framed the research question, 'What's wrong with educational TV programmes?', and I was able to enjoy the luxury of controlled enquiry, insulating myself from the problems of the classroom by studying articles on educational television in the quiet warmth of the polytechnic library.

The enquiry into educational television programmes proved an enjoyable activity, providing an intellectual extension to my everyday classroom experience and imbuing my self-image as teacher and researcher with a measure of importance. I approached the research with zeal; like a scientist trying to isolate a virus, I tried to identify 'the problem', the elimination of which would immediately improve my teaching. My findings from studying the literature were predictable: that the educational value of television depends upon the situation in which it is employed and the objectives governing its use.

Because the results of my literature review – that the context of TV use is all-important – had forced me back into reflecting on the classroom experience, I changed my question from 'What's wrong with educational TV programmes?' to 'How do students respond to TV programmes?' Although the research was back in the classroom, I still managed to avoid directly asking the crucial question which a teacher should ask: 'How can I use TV to create satisfactory learning experiences?' My research activity had become all-important; the search for discovering a universal truth about learning from TV had taken precedence over the immediate needs of the students in my classroom. I believe this occurred because my positive image of myself as an organized researcher might well contrast with the relatively uncontrolled classroom experience which I could expose by examining my teaching practice. Although I was not aware of this at the time, the need to maintain my self-image was paramount.

As I continued my research on how students responded to TV in the classroom, I planned a number of lessons in which TV would be used in a variety of different ways: full programmes, excerpts, programmes followed by excerpts. My stated intention was to examine, with the students, how TV had been used to assist their learning. Their reflections would then guide my subsequent use of TV. After four lessons of the research process I had arrived at a dead end. I did not have any firm data or outcomes, and I felt as if the research had driven a wedge between myself and my students. I was becoming conscious that my research was being done 'on' rather than 'with' the students; it was research to produce educationally respectable findings, yet paradoxically it ignored the students. In assuming the role of teacher-researcher, my research style reflected my teaching style: I was controlling and directing their classroom experience to produce the outcomes which I believed to be necessary. In retrospect, I realize that I had organized and paced lessons to ensure there was opportunity for 'useful' responses, and had planned the direction of their learning to incorporate all my research angles. In practice, I was not collaborating with the students; as in my everyday teaching, I took responsibility for the content and delivery of their lessons, and they could not adjust suddenly to becoming research partners when I decided to ask a 'research' rather than a 'subject' question, such as

Teacher: Do you think having a video was useful?
Student: Are we going on about your teaching methods now, not so much the actual programme?

I was so eager to justify myself as a researcher and a teacher that I managed to ignore weaknesses in my research behaviour. For example, I did not scrutinize the questions I asked – such as 'What themes do you think that I thought would arise from watching that?' – because, in my mind, it was only the answer to such a question that was important. I had assumed that because I had identified a classroom problem I could not be responsible for it. In retrospect, I can appreciate that I was desperately seeking support and reassurance both from the research and from the students, and I was manipulating the classroom experience to ensure such support was forthcoming. But this strategy was doomed, as 'data' from the research were partial and vague, although student response was becoming more direct: typically, 'While you're learning about teaching, we're learning nothing.' My attempt to create a controlled research environment by closely examining the students' response to television programmes while avoiding the teacher's behaviour had been manifestly unsuccessful.

By the end of this initial study I recognized that my classroom research was inconclusive, the students were generally unsettled and I was beginning to be conscious that I was guilty of interventions and manipulation. I was at a crossroads, and my personal response was to retreat and begin my journey again with another group. I thought that if I did not intervene quite as much in the next investigation I would end up with more conclusive results (or failing that, at least I would have comparative results) which would rescue my personal academic standing and self-image. Before reorganizing the research I would seek the sanction and support of my supervisor in discussing the future of my research.

Collaboration with experienced researchers

Seeking support and approval, I took my research record to my supervisor. He helped me reflect on my practice and provided support and direction. We reviewed a transcript of a discussion about classroom TV use involving myself and my students; he was able to view the transcript and the classroom objectively, and helped me to reconsider the possible effects of my behaviour. When I first analysed the transcript, I concentrated on student responses, ignoring the potential importance of my own comments. My supervisor drew attention to one of the questions which I has asked the class: 'What you remember is the pictures, not the commentary, is it not?' Until he pointed out the dubious research value of such a question, and also the effect such a teacher's question would have on the students, I had ignored my own comments, believing that it was only the students' replies that were crucial to answering the research question, 'How do students respond to educational TV?' In hindsight, I believe that because I always wanted the best for my students, I therefore had assumed that my classroom presence would always be positive and beneficial. Working on my own, I had unconsciously accepted that my questions were value-free, but reviewing the transcript of the discussion with the supervisor soon removed that illusion. As third party, he was not blinkered by being locked in the teacher–student relationship and was able to help me to reconsider my questions from a student's point of view. He drew attention to frequent examples of how, as researcher, I had used my advantageous status as a teacher to direct student responses – guiding answers, diverting comments and getting the students to guess 'what's in my mind'. My supervisor helped me realize that my enquiry was being limited by concern for my self-image. Having drawn my attention to considering the central question, 'What's really happening in the classroom?', he suggested that a study of classroom use of TV might be more productive if I organized a student-centred classroom activity without the teacher being present. I listened to what he said, while privately having reservations about letting both the students and the research out of my firm control.

Although I had an overall respect for his educational expertise, I felt that reducing my control over the students might be a recipe for anarchy in both classroom and research, and not practically possible in the 'real world' of teaching. Classroom control was important to me; I was haunted by the memory, from my early teaching days, of being embarrassed by my rowdy classes in corridors while experienced teachers averted their eyes from my red-faced discomfort. I had since evolved a natural style of control which I was reluctant to forsake.

The following day I had arranged a meeting with a media studies re-searcher. Whereas my supervisor had focused attention on my behaviour as a teacher, the researcher questioned me about my use of television in the learning experience. My initial problem had been that television did not stimulate student discussion and involvement. The researcher interpreted student reserve as a form of resistance to manipulation by the teacher whose own concerns are paramount. He explained how students are effectively excluded from 'Discussions where the teacher asks a question which really means, "Guess what I think the answer is . . . ?" What's the purpose of it? What are they going to do with the discussion, if and when they have it?' I was again confronted with the realization that my classroom problems were teacher problems, not television problems. As omniscient teacher I controlled, directed and took responsibility for what and how the students learned. Although I had an image of myself as a progressive, student-centred teacher, in reality this amounted to having a relaxed classroom, being sympathetic about homework deadlines and concentrating on subject areas of the syllabus which I thought the students would consider relevant. Obviously these concessions to 'progressive' education had merely made me a more tolerable didactic teacher, while simultaneously preventing me realizing that further change in my teaching was necessary.

Meanwhile, the research had to continue. The students had indicated, in informal discussion, certain areas in which some form of remedial action might be useful:

1 Students felt the teacher switching the TV set on and off to illustrate ideas was a barrier to their involvement.

2 The students did not always share the teacher's interpretation of a television programme.
3 The students perceived TV to be a passive experience.

The first two points could be seen as arising directly from a teacher-centred
classroom experience, and the final point was perhaps indirectly related to
this. Taken in conjunction with the conversations with both my supervisor
and the media researcher, they indicated that the question, 'What is the
teacher doing in the classroom?', must develop into a genuine enquiry; I
must risk discovering, 'What happens if students are given control of
their learning?' Thus, the next step of the research was to 'allow' the
students to work in small groups on their own with the TV and video
recorder and to audiotape them as they worked on an activity related to
the videotaped programme. This development was intended both to remove the self-important teacher-researcher, and also to explore what
happened when students themselves used the television in the classroom.
These activities were implemented and became the basis of the subsequent
research.

   Given my conscious and unconscious defensive strategies to maintain my
professional and personal self-image, it is worth reflecting on how I gained
the confidence to risk allowing both my students and my research to move
beyond my immediate control. A combination of factors contributed to my
decision. First, I had reluctantly come to accept that the research problem
was indeed a teacher problem; secondly, I could see no alternative direction in which the research could develop; and finally, the risk was a shared
responsibility – since I was acting on the advice of my supervisor, I felt he
would have some responsibility if the experiment 'failed' and the research
disintegrated. Furthermore, although I had regarded my exchanges with my
supervisor and the media studies researcher as generally critical of my
research practice, they both seemed convinced that more rigorous, student-
centred research in this area would be valuable, and this created a feeling
of worth which strengthened my resolve. In other words, collaborating with
others in examining my initial classroom research, especially in engaging in
frank discussion about my classroom problems, had been crucial to my
understanding of my teaching situation. Their constructive criticism had
challenged my assumptions, re-presented my practice in a way which helped
me recognize my defensive behaviour, and given me the necessary encouragement to take risks in the hope of improving my students' learning
experience.

   In the event, it was extremely easy to create a student-centred viewing
environment in the classroom. The major barrier was the psychological one
present in both teacher and students, that learning in the classroom is
dependent on the teacher being present. However, once I had the support
and guidance from my supervisor to absent myself from the classrooms, the

student groups were forced into taking responsibility for themselves and focusing on their own concerns.

I organized an activity-based viewing for three small groups of students. I audiotaped the groups and found that the resultant tapes and transcripts provided a refreshing insight into my students' experience which I could scrutinize and analyse without defensiveness. First attempts at analysis endeavoured to make sense of the transcripts by identifying recognizable categories of student behaviour. I noted the number of comments each student made, utterances referring to the task or to the television programme, and I also recorded the students' use of video recorder control features. However, this attempt to gain a 'scientific' respectability for my research was an inadequate record of the lively activity which had occurred in the groups. After consulting with my supervisor, I followed Barnes and Todd's (1977) example and abandoned a rigidly analytical system: 'In the analysis of in-formal discourse, it seems that one obtains reliability and inclusiveness at the expense of what intuitively seems to be meaningful.' Instead of looking *for* proof of learning, I adopted a more intuitive approach in which I tried to look *at* the experience from a student's perspective. I slowly reflected on each contribution, recreating the potential of each comment, and tried to empathize with the motivation of the speaker. This time I was not searching for proof of learning, I just wanted to understand what was 'going on'. This time, the text came alive.

It became apparent that there was a great deal of discussion between the students, most of which was relevant to the programme they had viewed. There was much evidence of valuable interaction: students were building, supporting, summarizing and clarifying each other's contributions. They seemed to be testing ideas against their own experiences and attempting to give abstract concepts a personal relevance. I realized that without my inhibiting presence, television could, and did, stimulate response and discussion.

I also began to be aware how the students' contributions were influenced by peer group pressure. Just as they frequently did not contribute when I was in the classroom, often the presence of other students within groups would affect individuals' responses. From the transcript I began to appreciate how students' behaviour, like teachers', is often heavily influenced by personal insecurity and the need to maintain a positive self-image. Students can and do learn from each other and can collectively develop ideas, but this is conditional on their having gained social approval as they explain the development of their personal thinking. In the time-consuming task of transcribing the audiotapes I had been able to listen at a deeper level to my students, and I realized that for the first time in my teaching career I was listening to students as self-conscious individuals, rather than as part of a class. In previous lessons I had been listening for 'relevant' contributions that were in accordance with my plans. Now I had awoken to their potential as individuals who were self-determining when released from my restrictive direction.

My work was now influenced by my developing consciousness of a new realm of classroom experience: classroom life as experienced by the students. My research had started with the teacher's problem – 'Why don't the students join in discussions after viewing TV as the teacher had anticipated they would?' Through working with other researchers I had begun to appreciate that my self-centredness as a teacher was a problem. I had now also come to realize that I must focus on the question which should have been my original concern – 'How can I understand, and consequently improve, the nature of the students' learning experience?'

Collaborating with the students

The next step was to work with the students to confirm that I had made reasonably accurate and honest interpretations of their behaviour. My discussions with students in the early part of the research had been a negative experience which had done little to improve either the teacher–student relationship or my knowledge of their learning experience. However, subsequent interviews about the group activity with five of the students – two pairs and one individual – stimulated some vigorous interaction and seemed to be mutually enlightening.

I could now identify certain factors which encouraged better communication between myself and my students and which helped us learn together. On a basic physical level, talking to two students rather than twelve is more comfortable. Three can sit as social equals around a desk: the teacher is not as physically dominant, it is easier to address the students as equals, and three participants adopt less confrontational postures than do a teacher and one student or a teacher facing a class. In the traditional teacher-led classroom situation a class member, when asked a question, seeks to understand, 'What's in the teacher's mind?' If the teacher doesn't know the answer, it is even more difficult for the student to guess and risk failure before his or her peers, so responses will tend to be inhibited. Moreover, when teachers are asking questions they are operating on two levels: content and the management of classroom interaction. A double concern with the outcomes of the exchange prevents them from really listening to the students' responses. It may be easier for the students, both physically and psychologically, to contribute when only two students are involved. Neither student is responsible for providing all the answers, yet each has more freedom to contribute to, and some control over, the direction of discussion. A student may well feel less vulnerable in a pair; there is less danger of looking a fool in front of the class or of upsetting norms, by, for example, seeming to be the 'teacher's pet'.

Underlying these practical changes was my altered attitude to the group. My relationship with the students was much more honest on these occasions, for I needed their guidance, not just their assent. The students appeared to appreciate my personal attention and interest. They were flattered that I had taken the effort to transcribe their conversations and showed both surprise and pleasure that their independent peer group discussion could have some worth. I think they enjoyed the novel opportunity to talk about themselves and their classroom experience, and they liked the role-reversal of being the expert and the source of knowledge in conversations with the teacher. Their enhanced self-esteem in turn made it easier for them to work with, rather than under, the teacher. I also believe that they appreciated my self-disclosure and trust in opening my teaching for inspection. This appeared to create an atmosphere which produced candid reflections. Central to the discussions were the transcripts, for they encouraged a focus of attention on an actual incident which was concrete and substantial and could be discussed and interrogated in depth. Just as, in an earlier transcript, my supervisor had focused on my behaviour, I was able to re-present their behaviour and thus help them develop a new consciousness about the underlying motives which had governed their individual contributions to the group.

Although the interviews with students were valuable in directing my attention to students' needs in the learning situation, the students still seemed somewhat inhibited in their responses. I had attempted not to ask questions, as questions between teachers and students can reinforce a power relationship. However, I found the one-to-one interview deteriorating into a question-and-answer session in which the student was obviously searching for the right answer. It was difficult to 'use' silence with one student, as she waited for me to direct the conversations; indeed, during one uncomfortable pause she asked, 'Is this what you wanted?' However, when she unexpectedly joined with another pair of students, she made a voluntary and major contribution about the difficulties of talking to a teacher in an interview: 'When [talking to] somebody you perceive to be intelligent, you automatically slip back into your working class way and you put them above you.' Even in an interview where a pair of students seemed to be enjoying contributing their thoughts and feelings, one of them justified their student-centred group activity because it helped her to 'give the answers the teacher wants'. The underlying expectations governing the student–teacher relationship derive from a lengthy educational experience which is heavily teacher-centred and cannot, it seems, be easily altered. There are, however, strategies that allow teacher and students to gain a greater consciousness of their interdependent roles in the learning process, and I discovered that such strategies only developed when I demonstrated respect for the students' experiences.

I also found the students' comments very helpful in intimating areas where my practice needed changing. Although interviews initially focused on television use, their reflections on my behaviour had wider significance. The students confirmed that groupwork was a positive experience as it removed my inhibiting presence: 'You don't like to comment when there's a teacher sat behind you . . . it just makes the atmosphere completely different.' Studying the transcript of the group viewing activity helped them to make comments about my behaviour which might otherwise have been considered inappropriate. The detached appraisal of their learning situation evoked comparisons between their science lessons and my traditional attempts at stimulating 'free' classroom discussions: 'You have to get on with the experiment, you can have a talk with your friends, it's not like this where everyone sits around and people are expected to contribute . . . . It's not for me.'

I began to appreciate my lack of empathy with students in failing to grasp the complex nature of their role. I used to think that I helped them develop ideas by providing the necessary links which would lead them to a conclusion. Discussions indicated that their tentative contributions and their gradual development of an idea reflected their need to maintain self-esteem, rather than their inability to make connections. Students know what they want to say but need constant reassurance before they will publicly own their ideas: 'I always think I've got to feed my ideas into people slowly [because] if my ideas are wrong it sort of comes back on me, doesn't it?'

The students also indicated that they were acutely conscious of the strategies they employed when engaging in discussion. As one student explained, 'I sort of pretend that I don't really know what I'm saying.' It is interesting to note that feeding ideas and pretended ignorance are also aspects of the teacher's repertoire. I became aware from our discussions that the private classroom experiences and insecurities of both teacher and students can be very similar. Yet unless I had created an environment conducive to mutual disclosure, I would have remained trapped in the accepted teacher–student relationship and ignorant of our common defensive behaviours. However, even since this discovery, I still occasionally find that under pressure I can retreat into a limited teacher's role, and my own needs blind me to the real needs of the students. A positive aspect of working with students was that they too seemed to learn from the discussion of the transcripts. The distance provided by the transcript allowed them to reflect objectively on their behaviour. They gained reassurance, not only from my interest, but also from their growing insights: 'So what we're doing really is building on what each other is saying and pushing it together to build one solid thing, so that in the end we come up with it.'

The interview situation also provided a supportive environment for the pairs of students to discuss the value of talking in the learning process: 'By speaking my thoughts out it clarifies them in my head and puts them in a logical order.' It helped them to realize that talking is often an 'unofficial' but very effective method of testing one's understanding: 'At break we'll ask each other, "But what did you put down?"' If the interviews confirmed that students' discussions did have an educational value and that they could engage in useful learning processes, it also brought home to me the fact that I have often prevented these useful exchanges, only allowing student-centred learning to occur in the short breaks between my teacher-centred activities.

To sum up, it was clear from the students' group activity that such student-centred activities gave them access to and control over the topic being studied and they became personally involved in evaluating the material. In a situation where they were given responsibility for understanding their own learning experience, they internalized the information and became more personally involved in subsequent discussions. Having learnt this, I attempted to create a student-centred activity as the main element in each weekly meeting of the class. I planned the activities to involve small, separate groups of three or four, and based the activities around a learning resource such as a videotape, audiotape or handout. I used to consider these as teaching aids, concerned with the delivery of information to students, but now I tried to adapt them as learning resources by making them more problematic – by removing conclusions, dividing the whole unit into parts for each group, or changing the context of the information. I also tried to maximize student involvement by asking groups to deliver their findings to the class while I sat with the remainder of the students. In general, I was confident that the classroom experience of myself and my students had been significantly improved by these changes in practice. But I must admit that as the exams drew near, I again found myself more frequently at the front of the class, finding reasons why a certain topic was inappropriate for a student-centred treatment. The pressures on me to ensure they passed their exams were again inhibiting my risk-taking.

Experience had shown me that students tended to pass their exams if subjected to my traditional teaching, but I could not be confident that their own learning was an adequate route to success. However, although a combination of pressures limited the degree to which I was prepared to change my established teaching behaviour, the fact that I continued to adopt a student-centred approach beyond the required research phase is a tribute to the support which I received within my own institution in an associated collaborative venture.

Working with a colleague in the institution

In the early part of my research I found that working with professional educational researchers provided challenging theoretical perspectives which both prompted me to examine my accepted teaching practices and indicated areas where progress was possible. My work with the students had revealed insights into their needs and had also encouraged me to continue with a student-centred approach. These collaborative relationships were further complemented by my work with a colleague, who provided the vital emotional support necessary if I was to continue taking risks in the classroom.

I was interested in involving our college staff development officer in my research, because in addition to his official role we enjoyed a good working relationship and I respected his considerable educational expertise. I asked Andy if he would analyse a tape transcript of the students' group activity and compare notes with me. I had originally thought that his extra perspective would add academic respectability to my research. In the event it became apparent that our discussions about the group activity became a vehicle for focusing on some key issues of our teaching lives.

For example, as we discussed the viability of encouraging student-centred activities and giving students the freedom to construct their own learning, Andy talked of the difficulties of letting go:

> In trying to work towards a very equal, open relationship between myself and my adult students, the most difficult problem I've got is me, it's me that I've got to work on, to be able to accept the implications of retreating from my pedagogic role . . . and the implications are that people are going to feel they can start saying things to me about what is going on in the group and how I'm doing things which most teachers never have said to them, because they never create a condition in which that is possible.

In this disclosure Andy confirmed what I had already experienced: that I could not effect improvement in the teaching and learning situation merely by changing my teaching methods or classroom management. It was also vital to recognize the need for some corresponding concession or adjustment in my teaching role and self-concept.

The true value to me of his comments arose from his trust in sharing his concerns. Throughout our discussion Andy practised effective staff development. By constantly disclosing his own problems, weaknesses and insecurities, he provided a safe context with which I could identify, upon which I could reflect and so learn. By emphasizing his belief that all teachers have problems – 'If somebody says they don't have any problems . . . either they're not telling the truth . . . or one of the most difficult things to deal with is, they might actually believe they've got no problems' – he helped remove pressures which prevented me from reflecting on the reality of my classroom. There was a significant difference between my collaboration with Andy and my general staffroom discussions with other teachers. Because of the impossibly high expectations placed on teachers, which we accept, I believe we develop strategies to deflect criticism and make ourselves invulnerable, both to external pressures and to self-doubts. We relate to supportive reference groups, using selected staff, friends, religious and political beliefs, even student responses (Nias 1986), to sustain ourselves. Many of our casual interactions with other staff are initiated and motivated by our need for support. Unfortunately, these changes can develop into a process in which we defend ourselves by seeing all our problems as the responsibility of others, be they bad management, inadequate resources or lazy students. My relationship with Andy led to a recognition that teachers do have problems and do need support but, as the teacher does affect the learning environment, one must continually focus on how teachers' behaviour might be changed in order to improve the learning situation. Thus, discussions which accept the teacher as a fallible human being can transcend the defensive limitations inherent in mutual staffroom support, and develop into constructive reflection.

When I began my meetings with Andy I felt that I was taking advice from a more experienced teacher. It was only after several meetings that I appreciated that Andy was also benefiting from our discussions. We then spent some time considering what we had both gained from our interaction and why the process of collaboration had been so mutually rewarding.

Having initially accepted an invitation to examine my teaching methods as part of his staff development role, Andy felt that our discussions became an extension of his normal role and he welcomed the opportunity to be involved in such a valuable aspect of staff development. He soon realized that he found our activity to be personally useful as well as helpful to my work. Although I initially interpreted his enthusiasm as politeness, I eventually became aware that examining a teachers' practice is rewarding for both participants. Investigating a teachers' behaviour forces one to reflect on one's own practice as one relates a given situation to one's own experience and educational values. Examination of another leads to awareness of oneself. A teacher who exposes his or her practice to criticism is demonstrating trust, which then invites reciprocal honesty and openness from the other. Thus a process of identification, self-realization, self-disclosure and feedback is stimulated in a non-threatening and productive environment. Andy further developed this notion that a collaborative relationship is mutually beneficial. Later he wrote:

> I began to realise that our discussions were fulfilling a need in me, a need for serious conversation, about, for example, learning. It was vital that in engaging in conversation with you, I could feel no inhibitions about exploring ideas of all sorts in a genuinely serious manner because I felt (and feel) you valued this also.

I have already touched upon the idea that teachers needing support form relationships and affiliate to reference groups which serve to maintain their self-image. While this support may help to insulate teachers from public criticism and private uncertainty, it appears that these measures of social approval still leave a need unfulfilled. It could be that Andy's desire for 'serious conversation about learning' represents a need to understand one's behaviour in the classroom, and realize one's vocational potential. Support that 'keeps you going' is not enough; one also has a need to know where one is going and why one is going there. I find this expressed need for 'serious conversation about learning' – a need which I share – to be an indication of the suppressed dimension of teachers' lives, hidden despite the fact that we seemingly engage in a great deal of work-related conversation.

After writing up a particularly stimulating meeting with Andy, I was surprised to realize that, although I felt I was getting major insights into teaching, all the important ideas that we had discussed were readily available in established educational literature. We had not discovered any 'new' universal truths about teaching. However, this did not reduce our satisfaction in making important discoveries about our roles in the learning situation; indeed, Andy saw these personal insights as being central to the collaborative process: 'It made clear the fact that it is possible to derive valuable ideas from our own minds.' Educational writings tended to use abstract terms which I could not relate to the crowded reality of my own classroom experience. In contrast, focusing on a precise classroom situation encouraged the use of a 'teachers' language'. We talked in terms of recognizable individuals in a familiar environment, while sharing an implicit understanding of the institutional constraints which influence actors in their settings. Collaborating within our institution allowed us to develop a language, a way of talking, that enabled us to gain a unique understanding of our own local situation. This language developed into a personal 'practical vocabulary' with which we could understand and discuss the everyday life of the classroom, which had previously not been articulated. The development of a specialized language also served to strengthen the developing relationship between us. This improved relationship created a climate that allowed further focusing on our classroom experiences, into increasingly sensitive areas. In short, the experience led to the creation of an appropriate language, and this language both symbolized our mutual understanding and acted as an instrument of analysis that allowed the classroom experience to be continually interrogated and personally realized.

Collaboration was not just a form of educational information exchange where techniques and experiences were traded, nor, despite my initial expectations, was it just a process through which the more experienced teacher could give guidance to his junior colleague. Andy believed that 'the outcome was much more than the two contributions because of the interaction between us,' and indeed this was true of my experience too.

Although our 'findings' were not original, our meetings gave me a conviction which helped support my continued risk-taking in the classroom. The very development of the conversations implied an affiliation of values and beliefs, which improved my self-esteem. Although we focused on commonplace classroom problems, our experience of investigating these problems was new to us. The effect of discovering something for myself created a powerful understanding that ensured the translation of the theoretical discussions about student-centred learning into practical experiments in the classroom.

Reflections

As I reviewed my research activity, I realized that the most constructive collaboration resulted from others having access to fragments of my practice. Productive reflections resulted from my supervisor analysing a transcript of my lesson, the media studies researcher viewing my lesson materials, and my colleague examining the transcript of the group activity. Successful interviews with students focused on an actual record of events, rather than a vague memory of what had happened in the lesson. Disclosure of one's classroom practice is invaluable because it creates a climate for trust and reflection. Sharing evidence of one's classroom activity invites relevant and immediate interaction. Some evidence of an actual incident provides a concrete focus for reflection from which shared ideas and principles will start to flow. Focusing on an aspect of a teacher's classroom life allows another to have access to the reality of that classroom, and provides a vehicle for debate. That debate can in turn use the classroom evidence as a means of developing a language about the teaching process that is meaningful to the collaborators. General debates about education often use abstract words which allow a variety of personal and possibly contradictory interpretations. By contrast, a concrete situation allows a variety of perspectives, all of which can be related back to the agreed meaning of the classroom event. I realized that as a teacher-researcher I was operating in two worlds: as researcher I claimed allegiance to 'democratic evaluation' (Walker 1985) in my research record, but I behaved as an autocrat in my classroom. My approach was guided by theoretical expressions which I found emotionally appealing, but which did not relate to my life in my classroom. So vague are the terms in which education and research are sometimes described that I did not realize that my teaching behaviour contradicted my stated research approach.

Consequently, experienced researchers were able to perform a dual function. First, when they had access to my practice, they acted as 'critical consultants', challenging my assumptions and making me acknowledge the effects of my classroom behaviour. They were then able to re-present my teaching to me, using the languages of both teaching and research. Working with these researchers informed my understanding of teaching by situating my daily practice within a wider educational context. They provided the opportunity for the 'reflection and confrontation' that Day (1987) claims is a necessary 'prelude to transformation'.

Day's experience of teachers researching their practice also led him to conclude: 'While most teachers are capable of reflecting on their perform-ances . . . the extent to which change will be implemented will be limited by the psychological and social environment or context in which the teachers work' (Day 1987: 212). My experience confirms his findings. Although external researchers were invaluable for provoking reflection and giving guidance, I still needed support in my institution before I would attempt extended risk-taking in my classroom. Thus it was important to have a sympathetic relationship with a colleague who encouraged my experiments to give students greater control over their learning. Within my college I felt there were strong pressures to conform to a traditional teaching role: management, staff and students all have expectations of desirable behaviour, and I felt my unorthodox approach could be viewed as a challenge by other staff. Research was already proving a solitary activity; I did not wish to be isolated as a deviant, as my classroom experiments challenged what I as-sumed were others' norms. Gaining the interest of a colleague who expressed 'a need to engage in serious conversation about learning' created for me a psychological and social environment conducive to risk-taking and the implementation of change.

My research activity involved progressive focusing from the outside of my behaviour as a teacher to its centre. Concern with a teaching aid – television – developed into an examination of how I used the medium, and this analysis of my teaching methods provided evidence of my role and my effects on the learning experience. The pattern of my collaborative relation-ships can also be seen as a movement towards the centre: from external consultation to partnership within the institution.

As I worked with others, I was enabled to reflect upon my practice and undergo a process of self-awareness. Continued refocusing of the research question in the light of my findings led to greater personal awareness and an understanding of the restrictive practices I had unconsciously assumed and inherited. This personal development stimulated a process of professional development as I attempted to change my practices and improve the classroom experience of my students. I discovered that I could only change the world around me by first learning how to change myself.

Part III

Feminist perspectives on working and learning together

Learning brings us together: the meaning of feminist adult education

Anne Spendiff

Introduction

The education of the woman should be always relative to the men. To please, to be useful to us, to make us love and esteem them, to educate us when young and take care of us when we grow up, to advise, to console us, to render our lives easy and agreeable – these are the duties of women at all times, and what they should be taught in their infancy.

(J. -J. Rousseau, quoted in Spender 1982: 104)

The struggle against the ideas of Rousseau, and other people like him who have sought to prescribe what women ought to be, is the feminist struggle. Or, to put it more positively, the feminist struggle is the struggle of women to decide for ourselves what we want to be.

This chapter is about how I am working with other women to make sense of feminism: it is about feminist research, feminist adult education and feminist ways of knowing and seeing the world. Sometimes I am tempted not to use the word; to compromise and to pretend that I am working for some kind of liberal notion of 'justice' or 'equality'. But when I do that I cannot convey the full meaning of what I am trying to do in my work, which is to place women and the experience of women centrally on the adult education agenda. This, for me, is what it means to do feminist adult education.

I am conscious of writing this chapter for educationalists who are interested in working and learning collaboratively, and who may at best be mildly interested in feminism, but who may at worst be actively hostile. I hope that my analysis of the problems of my own speciality will be of as much interest to a non-feminist as, say, special education is to a reception teacher, or the National Curriculum to a university teacher.

My analysis roots in patriarchy many of the problems and issues that I encounter. I find such an analysis helpful to me in the classroom because I can then look at my classroom problems and say, 'But what would be good for *women* here?' I have an explicit commitment to an ideology which offers a guiding principle to me in analysing the educational problems that I encounter. I do not offer the analysis as a panacea, but simply as a personal statement, incorporating my experience, my ideas and my feelings, and some of the ideas that I have found exciting in researching the literature of feminist education and in discussing the issues with colleagues and students.

Patti Lather defines the goal of feminist research as 'to correct both the invisibility and the distortion of female experience' (Lather 1986a: 68). I should like to apply that definition to all feminist processes, including education. One intention of this chapter is to explore the full meaning of such a definition, and through individual reflection to contribute to the building of collective meaning.

The rest of this chapter is divided into three sections. The first is a description of my work in women's studies in the north-east of England. The second is a review of the literature of women's studies. This is necessarily selective; I have chosen to describe and quote certain papers, and not others, largely because I have been able to connect what these writers have written with my own experience. Much of the literature is from North America, where women's studies appears to be more securely in the mainstream higher education curriculum than it is in the UK. Some of the writers are British, and some are West European. I have not attempted to review East European or Third World experience, largely because I cannot do it justice. I hope, however, that any reader who wants to pursue other areas can do so from the references I have given.

Next, I describe five of the current issues and problems that I experience in women's studies in more detail. The first problem is that of negotiating a curriculum, which I see as an essential part of working together with students, but which presents practical difficulties. The second concerns the place of emotion in the classroom. Feminism has sought to value the *whole* of women's individual selves and values feelings as highly as intellect, but there are special problems when we have to deal with emotional issues. This consideration leads into the other problems of student–tutor relationships, relationships with feminist colleagues and evaluation. These are issues that relate to the central theme of this book, and I describe some of my own experiences in learning and working with other women as students and colleagues. Finally, in the conclusion, I describe briefly the forces working to prevent women from changing our lives and relate the idea of political change to learning together in women's education.

New Opportunities for Women courses

I teach on the New Opportunities for Women (NOW) programme of courses sponsored jointly by Newcastle University's Centre for Continuing Education and the Northern District of the Workers' Educational Association (WEA).

The courses began in the early 1970s and their early history has been described by Aird (1985) and Tallantyre (1985). At first they were access courses into higher education or paid work, but they have developed considerably since their early days. I do not intend to describe their chronological development or speculate on the reasons for change, but to describe my experience of the courses now. North-east England in 1990 is very different from what it was in 1970, and the courses are designed to enable students with a variety of backgrounds and needs to meet the challenges that they face in their lives today. The courses are generally 20 weeks long and are for a half or a full day each week, within school hours.

Most of the courses are community-based, although courses on the university campus are still offered. Concessionary fees are available and crèches provided where possible, so that no woman should be barred from attendance. The courses are extremely varied. For example, a course held in Alnwick, a small market town in Northumberland, 25 miles away from the nearest higher education establishment, will be quite different from one held in Ashington, which formerly called itself 'the largest pit village in Europe', although it now has no pit. The needs of the women who look to Newcastle University's Centre for Continuing Education or the city's community education centres are different again. All the NOW courses are taught by part-time women tutors and the university has recently made available sums of 'development money' to pay tutors for course recruitment and educational development in their own communities. The sums of money are small, but they are an acknowledgement of the kind of work that is required to attract many women into higher education. It is inappropriate to expect such work to be carried out by staff based in a university that is both geographically and socially distant from many of the students.

The courses provided are suited to the localities, but they generally have at least two particular elements. The first is a women's studies element, which in recent years could have included politics, literature, health, science, writing or history. These are conventional academic disciplines, but the aim of teaching any of them, or any combination of them, in women's studies is to reclaim the culture of women for women. Thus, the experience of women is placed centrally in the courses so that students could be studying women writers, or the treatment of women by artists or politicians, or the experience of the students as consumers of the National Health Service.

The second element is still loosely called an 'opportunities' session, although its scope is generally wider than the word implies. Some students do want to explore opportunities for work or further study, but others want the time to consider and make sense of their own lives and their own feelings, and their own relationships. This wider approach has been developed by tutors in the belief that a focus on, for example, job-search skills will equip students only to search for jobs, whereas a focus on self-expression, confidence-building or assertiveness will equip them to make more positive and rewarding personal and social relationships within paid or voluntary work, the family, or further education. Another influence on tutors has been the increasing number of Wider Opportunities for Women or Restart courses provided by the Training Commission, Replan and other bodies which serve the job market. NOW courses have been broadened to cater for a different clientele: women who want to balance the variety of economic and social demands made upon them with their own personal and collective needs.

Generally, student-centred teaching methods are used, and the content of the courses also focuses on the experience of the women in the student group and of other women. I would therefore describe NOW courses as 'woman-centred', and concerned with the exploration of women's selves, as well as the acquisition of skills and knowledge.

My involvement: teaching in partnership

The courses are usually taught by pairs of tutors, and each pair develops its own way of working and planning the sessions, taking into account the students' needs and the time available. My own teaching has mostly been carried out in Northumberland, where I have taught women's studies now for five years, after having been a women's studies student myself.

Generally, in the courses I have taught, my partner and I have each taken responsibility for one or two periods of the time while the other supports or participates as a student. The periods could be anything: setting up a group exercise, brainstorming, studying an extract from a piece of writing, problem-solving, watching and analysing a video, or working out an assertive response to a particular incident. The broad contents of the course are negotiated with the students early on and the detailed activities worked out by the tutors, who try to provide a wide range of activities, combining material we have brought in with analysis of the students' own experience, and suiting the learning method to the content.

Teaching with a partner has advantages and disadvantages. On the one hand, it means that we can support each other, and that the students have two tutors from whom support can be sought. On the other hand, communications can break down, or tutors can find that, through no one's fault, their teaching methods or values are incompatible. Relationships between tutors have been explored in regular meetings of New Opportunities for Women tutors, which are described in the next section.

NOW course organization

Five years ago the WEA's tutor-organizer for women's education left and was not replaced. She was the only women's studies specialist with a tenured post in either of the sponsoring institutions, so neither Newcastle University nor the WEA currently has a women's studies specialist on its full-time staff. A number of part-time tutors and other activists have been campaigning to get the post filled, but we have been unsuccessful, although other staff have left and been replaced. This activism has formed us into a fairly close group, and the NOW tutors are now asked by the university to make re-commendations regarding resource allocation and staff deployment. The university employs part-time tutor counsellors whose job is to support tutors and organize staff development opportunities. One tutor counsellor has been allocated to the NOW tutors and our recommendation that the post should rotate within our group each year was accepted, although it is the only post that does rotate around tutors in this way. We chose to operate like this because we want our organization to be as democratic as possible; in 1989–90 the job was job-shared.

The NOW tutors collective meets for a whole day about twice a term. We carry out business, monitoring and planning the NOW programme and preparing submissions for the university. We discuss problems that arise and offer ideas and support to each other. Finally, we try to fit into each meeting discussion of a topic of general educational interest.

A small *ad hoc* group of NOW tutors has taken on the unpaid work of organizing residential training conferences for women working in women's education. One conference, held in cooperation with the North Western District of the WEA, which is based in Manchester, was held in the autumn of 1989. We raised £1700 from the WEA and from charitable donations to finance it. We did not need all the money we raised, so we organized a second conference for spring 1990. The question arises of whether training in women's education should be organized by unpaid workers and be dependent upon charitable funding.

My feelings about the whole NOW organization, and the amount of voluntary work involved, are complex. To begin with, I find the tutors' meetings useful and supportive, although not always easy. Sometimes difficult decisions have to be taken about resources or personnel, and I have oc-casionally wished that some autocratic leader could take both the decision and the responsibility. I have been conscious of the irony of being a mem-ber of a group of activists campaigning to put a woman in a position of power, where she could take autocratic decisions, while at the same time I have an ideological preference for the democratic structure we have developed. In some ways the NOW tutors collective is a preferable structure to the all-powerful full-time lecturer. We try very hard to share power among ourselves; we are a feminist group, in that we work for the well-being of women; and we represent a degree of workers' control. But some of these concepts are illusory. In fact, we have responsibility without rights, and influence, not power. The tutors are not paid for the work they do in the group (although the tutor-counsellors are); the university could disband us at any time; we depend on the support of a male head of division in the university, and a male district secretary and male tutor-organizers in the WEA. We have no negotiation rights as workers and no real control over resources as tutors.

Nevertheless, we have created a democratic feminist structure, which, for the moment at least, provides an opportunity for women to have some influence in a women's education programme, and enables us as workers to seek ideas and support. Women have learned to be opportunistic about such a turn of events, and to search for new strategies and structures when circumstances change.

The women's studies literature

What is women's studies? Definitions and themes

There do not appear to be agreed definitions of 'women's studies' or 'women's education'. Writers tend to establish their own definitions at the beginnings of their work. (Hughes and Kennedy 1985: 3; Schniedewind 1983: 261).

Bunch and Pollack (1983: xi) locate women's studies in the wider context of women's education, which they see as comprising:

- The teaching of specific skills (from reading and writing to computer technology and film-making) and passing on of information to students that will help them to survive better in the existing culture while working to change it.
- The development of feminist consciousness and the educating of women specifically about the women's movement, about women's diverse individual achievements and cultural heritages, and about various feminist theories and strategies for change.
- The creation of space, the encouragement of desire and the provision of tools for women to develop their ideas, theories, art, research and plans so that the body of feminist knowledge and action is expanded.

My own definition of women's studies corresponds to Bunch and Pollack's second component of women's education, although I believe that all three components overlap, and I feel that none of the three is explicit about the particular features of teaching methods that other writers see as inherent in women's studies.

Renate Klein (1987), for example, summarizes some of the writing on women's studies, and chooses to present not definitions, but an analysis of themes that she recognizes as appearing frequently in articles on women's studies. These themes relate to feminist teaching method, which she calls 'gynagogy' (noting that a pedagogue was originally a man in charge of boys). The themes are:

- Consciousness raising, feminism's own strategy, which I shall discuss later.
- Interactive learning, which is seen as empowering for women because it is active rather than passive and because it encourages women to cooperate with each other rather than to compete.
- Being 'other' in the women's studies classroom – i.e. a recognition of *differences* between women due to racial origin or sexual preference. (Klein's literature review relies heavily on the US experience. From a British perspective, I would add class to this list).
- A concern with teacher–student power difference, which I shall also discuss later.

Klein summarizes Schniedewind's (1983) article on suggested process goals for gynagogy, which include a number of goals implicit in the main theme of this book: development of a classroom atmosphere of mutual respect, trust and community, shared leadership, and cooperative structures. Other goals are the integration of cognitive and affective learning, and the necessity for action on the part of students. Klein concludes:

> If Women's Studies is to be more than another discipline or 'just' feminist scholarship integrated in conventional disciplines, the distribution of knowledge requires a teaching practice which fulfills its original promise to the Women's Liberation Movement to empower women intellectually, politically and personally. In the poetic words of a song by the British Greenham Common Peace Women: 'It's not just the web – it's the way we spin it; it's not just the struggle – it's the way we win it.'
>
> (Klein 1987: 202)

Attempts such as these to assert what women's studies is and how it is taught are paralleled by feminist critiques of conventional adult education pedagogy.

Pat Mahony, for example, criticizes conventional academic courses (including some women's studies courses) for contravening some basic feminist principles; she says methods are hierarchical, with power vested in tutors who are seen as 'experts' while students are seen as ignorant. She says that the personal experience of students is not valued and that pre-established content can lead to 'destructive, conflict-ridden group relationships' (Mahony 1988: 104). Finally, Mahony describes her attempt to establish a feminist teaching method.

In contrast, *Learning the Hard Way* (Taking Liberties Collective 1989) describes the experience of women in education largely in the words of the students. A socialist feminist theory is derived; that is, the women's experience of class rather than gender is seen as the central determinant of their oppression. The book begins with descriptions of students' own lives, and goes on to describe educational experience at school and in adulthood, finally describing students' women's education classes. Here are two examples of the student quotations, which indicate the oppressive nature of some educational experiences:

> After cookery lessons the boys would hang around the classroom door waiting for culinary handouts. They preferred samples from those whose cooking was best, so even cookery lessons became a test or competition for their benefit.

> If inadequate explanation or unnecessary use of long words widened the gulf between lecturer and student, the matey approach did not always help to narrow it. Speaking of one Marxist critic, Althusser, one of them said, 'So what if he bumped off his old dear?'
> (Taking Liberties Collective 1989: 58 and 97)

Thus, some writers have chosen to define women's studies fairly specifically, while others choose to describe it, either in their own words or in the words of their students, sometimes choosing to describe it in terms of what it is *not* – that is, patriarchal education. My personal preference is for the description of what women's studies *is*, and speculation about what it might be, although I understand that feminist education exists within a political context, and that feminist educationalists are engaged in a constant struggle both for resources and for academic freedom. In such circumstances a critical perspective is necessary, but so is vision. Marcia Westkott says: 'We know from our classes in Women's Studies the importance of pushing our criticism past itself to the visions that the criticism suggests . . . . To push beyond criticism, however, is not to relinquish it, but to hold it in tension with vision' (Westkott 1983: 213).

The politics of women's studies

Marcia Westkott is one of the writers who emphasize that the scholarship of women's studies is linked to the aims and visions of the feminist movement, and to ending the devaluation, subordination and oppression of women (Westkott 1983: 210; see also Rutenberg 1983; Klein 1987). There are a number of aspects to this political position. To begin with, there are similarities between the feminist political strategy of collective consciousness raising and the methods of liberatory education, such as student-centred learning and learning from experience. Secondly, several writers identify women's studies as a strategy for change from which other critical educational movements can learn. Thirdly, there is the issue of how we can work together to defend women's studies at a time of financial and cultural restriction. Finally, there is the question of men's collaboration in women's studies.

Consciousness raising has been described and defined by feminist writers. Terry Wolverton defines it as a fairly rigid process of witnessing and analysis:

> Each woman gets an equal amount of uninterrupted time to speak about her own experience. Women then discuss and analyse both the commonalities and differences expressed. It is a process rooted in the belief that the theory we develop must come from our real, lived experience.
>
> (Wolverton 1983: 188)

The use of the plural here is significant, for it is only in analysing experience *together* that women begin to learn that our experience of oppression is collective and widespread, that it is valid as a political entity, and that it is not an individual shortcoming.

Hester Eisenstein emphasizes the collective validation process and relates it back to the individual:

> What women had to say about the details of their daily lives, about their personal experiences and histories, mattered, it had significance, and above all, it had validity. This meant that the source of authority, of legitimacy and validity about the lives of women, and the significance of what they experienced was the individual herself.
>
> (Eisenstein 1984: 37)

Both writers indicate that consciousness raising also leads to and supports collective political action for women. It is a process that connects the study and validation of experience with analysis and action, and women's studies tutors can use this connection with effect in an educational context.

Sandra Bartky reminds us that learning about the extent of women's oppression can also be painful:

> In sum, feminist consciousness is the consciousness of a being radically alienated from her world, and often divided against herself, a being who sees herself as victim and whose victimisation determines her being-in-the-world as resistance, wariness and suspicion ... that feeling of alienation ... is counterbalanced by a new identification with women of all conditions and a growing sense of solidarity with other feminists. It is a fitting commentary on our society that the growth of feminist consciousness, in spite of its ambiguities, confusion and trials, is apprehended by those in whom it develops as an experience of liberation.
>
> (Bartky 1975: 437–8)

Renate Klein summarizes a number of articles on the uses of consciousness raising in the classroom. Together we are able to understand and
theorize from our own experience and to build confidence. Feminist critics
of consciousness raising feel that it places too much emphasis on individual
self-expression and insufficient emphasis on analysis and the exploration
of the experiences of women outside the group, in the form of historical,
literary or other material (Klein 1987). I experience difficulty with this balance
myself, and I shall explore it further later. I am sure, though, that women's
studies *must* incorporate consideration of the possibilities of change at both
personal and social levels, and this brings me to the second aspect of the
political theory of women's studies: women's studies as a strategy for personal
and political change.

Pat Mahony is adamant: 'If Women's Studies claims to be feminist then it
has to be committed to change' (Mahony 1988: 105). Florence Howe points
out that all teaching is a political act because someone is 'choosing, for
whatever reasons, to teach a set of values, ideas, assumptions and pieces of
information . . . . To include women with seriousness and vision and with
some attention to the perspective of women as a hitherto subordinate group
is simply another political act' (Howe 1983: 110).

Patti Lather goes further. Using concepts and words derived from the
work of Antonio Gramsci, she proposes that women's studies, in its attempts to be democratic, is also a model for other critical and liberatory
educational programmes:

> While critical theorists of the curriculum speak of the importance of
> counter-hegemonic examples . . . the significant example of curricular
> change through women's studies goes unnoticed.
>   Women's studies has some potent weapons in its counter-hegemonic
> arsenal. We know that developing people's self-activity is essential. We
> have developed leadership patterns that do not make others feel in-
> adequate or uninvolved. We know the importance of ideological tools
> – the tools that negate the power of those who determine and define
> what is real and legitimate . . . . We know that the task is self-education
> through praxis: knowing reality in order to transform it.
>   (Lather 1984: 50 and 58)

Unfortunately 'those who determine and define what is real and legitimate'
are keen to hold on to their power to do so and resist the challenges that
women's studies presents.

The third political aspect to women's studies concerns its defence within
institutions that we perceive as hostile. This defence and the struggle for
resources for women is illustrated in the story of every women's studies
class that exists, and strategies differ from place to place. *The World Yearbook of Education* (Acker 1984) devoted itself to a set of review articles

describing the development of girls' and women's education all over the world, but notes that in the UK 'there has been little dialogue . . . on the question of building a trans-disciplinary [women's studies] movement' (Klein 1984: 300). I would suggest that one of the reasons for this is that women have had to be flexible – not to say anarchistic – in the way we organize ourselves at a local level.

Worldwide, there is a very real debate about how far feminists can work within the system (called 'mainstreaming' in the USA) without compromising our beliefs. *Learning Our Way* (Bunch and Pollack 1983) contains accounts of the ways women in the USA are choosing to defend their provision. *New Futures: Changing Women's Education* (Hughes and Kennedy 1985) in-cludes a collection of British case studies, almost all of which are of pro-vision in voluntary organizations, which are seen to be more amenable to radical ideas than the state sector.

When I read the case studies in these books, and when I talk to other women's studies tutors, I am struck by the initiative and resourcefulness we all demonstrate in just keeping our programmes going. Whether we work inside or outside of the educational establishment, there always seems to be a struggle. Every tutor, every class, has to develop its own political strategy for survival, whether in New York State University (Bunch and Pollack 1983: 59) or in the Totnes Women's Centre in South Devon (Hughes and Kennedy 1985: 104). I am not sure, from my reading, that there is any collective global or national strategy that will preserve women's studies as a properly resourced discipline, within the control of women. Neither has my experience led me to adopt a strategic position, other than one of expediency. I believe that these case studies indicate that women have a rich variety of collective strategies that can be adopted at different times and in different circumstances, whereby money can be obtained from the likeliest source for a project that will answer as many needs as possible of an optimum number of women, involving the fewest possible compromises of feminist principles. Probably, within all these variables, every feminist would strike a different balance, and this can make collective working difficult at times. Sometimes feminists have to work hard for unity, but we are also flexible and this flexibility can mean that our political oppo-nents will strike us down and win one victory, only to see us rise up with a different structure, a different strategy and new money, somewhere else.

The fourth political aspect of women's studies concerns the role of men. Feminists' political opponents are generally men who are in positions of power, rather than in the equal relationships which foster collaboration. However, we are often asked whether men can play a *positive* role in women's studies. More often, we are told that they can.

Bunch and Pollack describe their difficulties in working with men as students:

Men have little to contribute to the exploration of women's realities because they haven't experienced them. We understand that men need to learn that their lives do not reflect the whole world, but even those men who sincerely wish to do this find it difficult to accept a perspective that challenges their use of privilege to oppress women.

(Bunch and Pollack 1983: 65)

If men cannot learn about women's experience of oppression, it is questionable whether they can teach it. Hughes and Kennedy address the issue of male tutors in women's studies, and say that even sympathetic men are unable to transcend deep-seated male-centred opinions and ideas:

So we do not think men could teach feminist studies to women but they can and should take on the study of gender and sex roles and relationships throughout the curriculum. They should study and teach what the implications of a feminist perspective are for them.

(Hughes and Kennedy 1985: 27)

I would add to this positive view of what men can do in supporting women, that they could question sexist assumptions and statements made by their own male colleagues. In short, men cannot know about women's oppression, but they can speak of what they do know, which is men's sexism. Robert Bezucha (1985) has described what it is like to be a man teaching in women's studies, but I am not convinced that his introspection has benefited women in any way.

Of all the possible compromises I might make in my teaching, I will not compromise on the principle that women's studies is *for women*, not because we need some kind of special or remedial education to help us cope in the world of men, but because we 'have our own history and culture to reclaim, our own knowledge to create, our own skills to identify and use and our own political priorities to attend to' (Taking Liberties Collective 1989: 153). I can see no end to the tension between men and feminists or men and women's studies. While feminists challenge men's power, both institutional and personal, men will resist that challenge and there will be a complex picture of conflict, accommodation, reform, respect, collaboration, fear, distrust and support. If women's studies truly is to be the educational branch of the women's liberation movement, then the content, method and organization of women's studies will reflect the political realities of that movement, and those of us who are active in women's studies teaching are, by definition, political activists, whether we like it or not.

The politics of women's studies is reflected in the difficulties experienced by tutors in the classroom, and the final section of this paper reviews some of the issues that I have found particularly difficult.

Issues in women's studies

I have identified the issues outlined here because they have presented me with problems in teaching. I hope that educationalists who are not in women's studies can identify with the *teaching* problems, and might be interested in my analysis of them as rooted in patriarchy and calling for feminist solutions. Two of the problems relate to teaching content: the difficulties of negotiating a curriculum, and the use of emotion in the classroom. The third and fourth are concerned with the nature of tutor–student relationships and relationships between feminist colleagues, and the last with evaluation.

A negotiated curriculum in women's studies

Feminism's concern to empower women is consistent with the educational practice of a negotiated curriculum. The central problem here is negotiating around topics that students do not even know exist. Dale Spender describes the suppression of women's ideas:

> The simple answer to my question – why didn't I know about the women of the past who have protested about male power – is that patriarchy doesn't like it. These women and their ideas constitute a political threat and they are censored. By this means women are 'kept in the dark,' with the result that every generation must begin virtually at the beginning, and start again to forge the meanings of women's existence.
>
> (Spender 1982: 13)

Spender's whole book is a reclamation of women thinkers. Other writers have reclaimed for women's studies women in history (Rowbotham 1977), in literature (Showalter 1978), in philosophy (Vetterling-Braggin *et al.* 1977) and in other disciplines (for example, Dubois *et al.* 1985). Evidence of the boom in women's studies publishing and bookselling can be seen in most large bookshops.

Women's invisibility in conventional scholarship presents particular problems for curriculum negotiation. For example, students may not know that women in nineteenth-century US anti-slavery campaigns became feminists in very similar ways to the women of 1968, as a reaction against orthodox political activity. They are unlikely to ask to study nineteenth-century American feminism, because feminism is popularly seen as a recent phenomenon rather than a bona fide – and very ancient – perspective on the world.

A further problem arises when students are unused to democratic participatory decision-making and expect, for example, to be told what they need to know. The process here is even more complex: tutors have to equip

students with just enough information to enable them to make real democratic choices regarding their own education, and we also try to foster the
belief that, if liberation is to be real, individual students can make their own
choices without appeal to a higher authority or ideology.

In the north-east we generally offer short, taster courses over the summer
months, and individual tutors find their own ways to enable students to
control their education. Generally in a NOW course I will plan the first half-
term with three or four taster sessions and introduce ideas about how the
group can operate and take decisions democratically. I then attempt to
negotiate the rest of the course. This presents further problems when the
university asks for a 'syllabus' or wants me to say in advance what 'subject'
I will teach. Nevertheless, I feel that it is necessary to maintain the position
that women's studies *is* a subject, and that a negotiated curriculum is preferable to a prescribed one. This means that I continually have to defend the
way I teach NOW courses, and the way I prepare for them.

The expression of emotion in the women's studies classroom

I have already described consciousness raising and indicated how it can be
used in the classroom to validate and analyse women's feelings and experience, and how it can lead to action. Gearhart says that:

> Early on the Women's Movement challenged the 'myth of the half-
> person', i.e. the existence of something called 'feminity' and something
> called 'masculinity' in human beings, and it deplored society's over-
> valuing of rational ('masculine') functions (objectivity, logic, analysis,
> linearity) to the near exclusion of nonrational ('feminine') functions
> (subjectivity, emotionality, intuition, synchronicity).
>
> (Gearhart 1983: 4)

Tally Rutenberg emphasizes that traditional 'objective methodologies' have
served to oppress women:

> Theories developed by traditional academicians and physicians [of the
> nineteenth century] held that 'hysteria' was the disease which stemmed
> from a woman's inability to accept her God-given, biologically man-
> dated role as wife and mother. Had these theoreticians listened to the
> feelings of women about their lives as wives and mothers, had they
> not been exclusively academic in their approach to 'hysteria', and
> were they not without a vested interest in the subjugation of women,
> their theories would have been based on fact rather than on objective
> fantasies.
>
> (Rutenberg 1983: 74)

Women's studies serves to reverse the divisive nature of the traditional
disciplines, and to assert a more holistic view of women's identity, but it

recognizes that to do so is painful. Sandra Bartky's view on this was described earlier, and is supported by Barbara Hillyer Davis: 'It is a commonplace among us that studying women is a painful experience for women, and that Women's Studies classrooms should provide an environment in which women can support one another through this pain' (Davis 1983: 92).

Eileen Aird draws upon psychoanalytic theory to assert that women have great capacities for nurturing relationships. She believes that in NOW courses women use these nurturing capacities to support other women, rather than the men and children whom we usually support. Generally, women's dependency needs are unmet, and this can be remedied in women's education (Aird 1986). This view is supported by Culley and Portuges, who believe that the women's studies classroom

> creates a highly charged, fantasy-laden recapitulation of the mother/
> daughter nexus, that life-long relationship imbued with a complex
> and contradictory dynamic of individuation and fusion, reminiscent of
> the infant's needs for separation and differentiation from the mother.
> (Culley and Portuges 1985: 16)

My experience supports this description of women's studies classrooms as 'highly charged'. The content of women's studies is very powerful: women are confronted with the fact that across generations and across cultures other women have felt the same anger and pain, and suffered the same oppression and abuse. The sudden realization that a student is not alone in her feelings of alienation and fear can produce a very emotional response and tears – and laughter – are common in women's studies classrooms.

Our teaching methods also facilitate the expression of emotion. Tutors generally control the learning environment so that women will not feel intimidated, and will feel confident enough to express hopes and fears, and to question. This calls for special skills from the tutors. We need to be sufficiently skilled in facilitation so that we can encourage cooperation and support within student groups. We need to be able to deal tactfully with emotional issues, such as abortion or rape. Frequently students confide in tutors individually and we need to have counselling skills to cope with this. In particular, tutors need to have a woman-centred view of emotional problems. By this, I mean a belief that, for example, it is the perpetrator of rape or sexual harassment or domestic oppression who is at fault, and not the victim. Tutors can be trained in these skills and attitudes and need time to consider the ethical and personal questions that are raised in such processes. The problems of using subjective feelings in the classroom are not insurmountable, although the commitment of the 'providing institutions' to training is questionable, as I have indicated above.

For me, the main problem is in integrating the expression of feeling with more conventional study, such as reading or problem-solving. Clearly, if a student has disclosed some experience of abuse, it is inappropriate to move rapidly on to the next exercise. Generally, I would allow the group to deal with such an occurrence, and facilitate the exchange of ideas and feelings that are expressed, no matter how long it takes. In my experience, groups generally deal with disclosures themselves provided that they have the time to do so. I believe that as tutors we have a responsibility to ensure that each woman has an opportunity to say what she feels and does not go away with unexpressed feelings of pain or anger. However, less shocking disclosures can also be made, and after these I have had to judge the correct time to move on. Breaks for coffee give students the time to talk in pairs or small groups about an issue, and can remove the item from a group agenda and on to a more personal one, consistent with Eileen Aird's idea that students' dependency should shift from tutors on to other students:

> Initially it is likely that the tutor will have to hold the dependency of the whole group and of individuals. As the weeks go by, and trust grows among the women a network of responsive caring will be established which diffuses and meets individual needs.
>
> (Aird 1986: 221)

Every year I am amazed that this is what happens, that students almost always begin courses with anxiety and complete them with confidence drawn from the support of other women. I am convinced that an essential part of this process is the validation of students' feelings, as well as the development of cognitive skills.

The role of the tutor in women's studies

Feminism's concern with holism has led feminists to question not only the emotional–intellectual divide, but also the divide between objectivity and subjectivity. Barbara du Bois, in her essay advocating that feminist scholarship should be 'passionate scholarship', says: 'We are observer and observed, subject and object, knower and known. When we take away the lenses of androcentrism and patriarchy, what we have left is our own eyes, ourselves and each other' (du Bois 1983: 112).

This view is inconsistent with the traditional idea of a pedagogue who is a 'knower' and imparts his knowledge to the ignorant. In the classroom I try to facilitate an understanding of women's shared experience – and this includes my own. However, I am aware that, as a paid tutor, I have special responsibilities for both the content and the process of the course. I do have some knowledge about women's lives that my students have probably been denied, as I outlined earlier. And I also have an analysis that they may not share. I feel that some of my responsibilities ought to be shared by the student group. For example, I want the group to respect the needs of other people, like crèche workers, and to respect each other's needs, for example, by listening or not dominating the discussion. Ultimately, however, the responsibility for these things is mine, and I have the power to take that responsibility. I choose to share both power and responsibility when I can, although this is not as easy as it may seem. My research into my own teaching has forced me to think hard about the power I have as a tutor. I have learned that I frequently take power unconsciously – perhaps by standing up or moving around the room, things that students do not do, or by giving out a handout, or even just by picking up a felt-tip pen. In an effort to eliminate such behaviour, I over-compensated and left the room during a curriculum-negotiation exercise, only to discover that a powerful sub-group of students took control and other, quieter students did not get a fair hearing.

Barbara Hillyer Davis (1983: 94) identifies a number of roles that tutors in women's studies can adopt:

- *Superwoman*, which is a 'feminisation of the professorial role: by adding responsibilities for interpersonal relationships to our work as discussion leaders, evaluators, role models and paper graders, we "humanise" the classroom.' Students can force tutors into this position because they *expect* tutors to behave in a certain way, so tutors 'play the role of superwoman, killing ourselves with overwork and denying the students responsibility for their own relationships.'
- *Wife*, which is 'more insidious. "Let me help you be more comfortable," we suggest. "You're O.K., dear, and I will work to reassure you."'
- *Mother*, similar to wife. 'The catch to these two solutions is that the proper correlative roles are those of husband and child, neither of which seems appropriate to the feminist classroom.'

Ultimately, Davis believes that tutors and students should be sisters:

> What I know about feminist process makes me feel an obligation to renounce the professional role, to serve instead as a role model for sisterhood, disclaiming any stance of superiority and presenting my-self as one who learns instead of teaching.
>
> (Davis 1983: 91)

She notes, however, that many students are more comfortable in a traditional classroom relationship, and she tries to balance the different pressures upon her.

I too am conscious of the need to balance all the pressures, and I make judgements intuitively about which role to adopt in the classroom. I believe, however, that the ultimate barrier between tutor and student is not superior knowledge or responsibility for the dynamics, but the fact that as a tutor I am unable to have my dependency needs met in the classroom. I have never been able to disclose *real* problems in class sessions, and when I have tried to seek support from students in breaks, or even when courses have finished, I have never received the kind of support I wanted. Thus, while I can be sister or mother in the classroom, I can never be a child, and for me that is the ultimate barrier to equality between tutor and students in women's studies.

Feminist working relationships

Feminism forces women to question relationships between tutors and students, and it also forces us, as tutors, to ask fundamental questions about how we work together, and about the nature of work itself. For me, the major objectives are that we work democratically and supportively. I have already described how we generally work in pairs and how the NOW tutors' group functions. Many of our problems can be overcome through talking and sharing and improving communications generally; this is perhaps a conclusion that many educationalists would have predicted.

There are two areas where I would say my consciousness about feminist working has been raised in the tutors' group. The first has been in dealing with my feeling that my teaching is in some way inferior to that of my partner. I have felt this with different partners and in different circumstances. In the tutors' group it became evident that all of us felt this at times, and we concluded that such feelings were not the result of an objective evaluation of our teaching, but of some kind of internalized sense of inadequacy, which we attributed, rightly or wrongly, to patriarchy. Thus, I have, in our group, been able to raise my own consciousness about the position of women in academia, and have been able to see that the problem that I thought was mine alone is, in fact, part of a pattern of feeling that is common and deserving of further analysis.

The second area that I have had to work on has been my tendency to 'mother' my colleagues and not to allow them to take on full responsibility for their own actions. If a colleague has confided some anxiety or stress to me, I have been inclined to protect her from my own worries or feelings of overwork because I have not wanted to bother her with my problems. I have then become resentful, and kept this feeling to myself as well.

I do not see any particular solutions to these problems beyond airing them and placing them on agendas. I learned about the teaching process during 18 years of conventional education. Clearly, I have a lot to unlearn about education, about being in 'authority' as a professional teacher and about being a supportive colleague. In the NOW tutors' group the con- sciousness raising process has worked for me, in that I have been able to examine subconscious processes and to re-learn ways of thinking and behaving that are more honest, so that I can express and explore feelings of inadequacy and resentment in a supportive atmosphere. Only when that is done will I be able to create new, feminist, ways of relating to colleagues and students in the classroom.

Measuring our achievement

Barbara Hillyer Davis points out the difficulty of being both a sister to our students and a 'paper-grader' (Davis 1983: 94). It has never been our practice, on NOW courses, to offer grades or certificates. At the beginning of courses we ask students what they want to achieve, and those who want to return to formal education are particularly encouraged to do written assignments which receive comments, not grades. We also offer to write references.

Students have not expressed dissatisfaction with this arrangement, but there is pressure upon us to carry out profiling, and I feel we may have to re-assess our policy. Some women's studies courses, of course, require some kind of assessment of student performance, and this is probably an area where different tutors would make different compromises between compliance with institutional requirements and the feminist principle of not oppressing other women. For myself, I would like to maintain the position that I will not judge the achievements of women and dub them successes or failures as long as we live in a society that labels women as failures, no matter what we do (Spender 1983: 29). I feel, however, that the rather liberal approach that we adopt on NOW courses, of allowing students to set, assess and re-assess their own personal criteria for success or failure, has led us into difficulties with the providing institutions. These subjective student assessments are considered to be less valid than the ultimate quantitative measure of adult education success in a market economy: numbers of students paying a full fee. If we can keep this figure high, then the NOW courses are safe. The required figure, of course, is set according to objective criteria. It varies from time to time and place to place.

Women's studies tutors, locally at least, have not had the opportunity to research and develop other means of assessing the success and failure of our courses. Neither have we had the necessary support to evaluate our own performances. Any research that has been done has been on the initiative of individual tutors. My own research has been carried out as part of a Newcastle upon Tyne Polytechnic MA in Educational Development.

Becoming a student again has enabled me to learn ways of researching what I do, and has given me access to the library facilities that have enabled me, among other things, to write this chapter. One of my discoveries has been the amount and quality of feminist social science research that is being carried out (e.g. Eichler 1980, 1988; Roberts 1981; Mies 1983; Stanley and Wise 1983; Acker 1984; Lather 1986a,b; Smith 1987). I have, however, looked in vain for evidence of this type of research being carried out to assess and evaluate women's education. I suspect that such research would represent a triple non-conformity – of course content, teaching method and research methodology – and hence might be very difficult to implement in a conventional educational institution, where at least some conformity is probably required to guard against total alienation. Whether this analysis is correct or not, I have not been able to find a model for investigating my practice that seems to me to be consistent with feminism, so I am having to develop my own methodology of research into women's education.

Conclusion

Simone de Beauvoir said, 'One is not born, but rather becomes a woman' (de Beauvoir 1960: 295). She argues that it is not biology but civilization that determines our identity. Whether or not I entirely agree with this, I do believe, as a feminist, that contemporary British society does distort women's identities to the extent that I, at least, have to look very deeply inside myself in order to discover what is natural and what is learned behaviour. One way in which I can do this is in the company of other women, where we can give and receive support and share analyses, both individual and collective, about our own identities as women. De Beauvoir recognizes that women are frequently isolated from each other, living 'dispersed among the males, attached through residence, housework, economic condition, and social standing to certain men – fathers or husbands – more firmly than they are to other women' (de Beauvoir 1960: 19). Women's education gives students the opportunity to overcome our isolation, question established 'wisdom' and determine what we may choose to become for ourselves.

Rousseau's statement, quoted at the beginning of this paper, may appear rather quaint in the 1990s, but pressures do still exist on us to be good mothers, not to raise delinquent children, to return to paid work, to grow old gracefully, to run voluntary organizations, to join trade unions, to establish small businesses, to remain sexy for our husbands and to prepare *cordon bleu* meals. The role models the media present us with vary from the eternal youth of Joan Collins to the assertiveness of the former Prime Minister. If our bodies are the right shape, we can appear half naked in newspapers on family breakfast tables. Some of us can be astronauts, war correspondents or saviours of the dying in Calcutta. I believe that for most women these are oppressions, not opportunities, and that simply trying to establish our own identities and take control of our own lives in the face of all this is a major political – and collective – task.

This chapter has been an attempt to describe my experience of addressing that task through women's education. I have located that description in my local situation and in the literature of feminism. More particularly, I have tried to emphasize throughout the need for women to work together to learn about ourselves and to develop our own educational methods and our own political strategies. I have identified some problems, which I see as arising from learning in a patriarchal society that divides and isolates women and denies us not only knowledge of our whole individual selves, but also consciousness of ourselves as an oppressed group. I see women's education as one way of bringing us together, and validating our individual and collective experience.

Sometimes I wonder what all the fuss is about; all we are trying to do is to develop ways of offering education to women. But, as I have indicated, almost every feminist education project has its story of power struggles to tell. The poet Adrienne Rich has asked:

> What does a woman need to know? Does she not, as a self-conscious, self-defining human being, need a knowledge of her own history, her much politicized biology, an awareness of the creative work of women of the past, the skills and techniques and powers exercised by women in different times and cultures, a knowledge of women's rebellions and organised movements against our oppression and how they have been routed or diminished?

> (Rich 1985: 24)

Surely, that is not asking for too much. Rich continues:

> Without such knowledge, women live and have lived without context, vulnerable to the projections of male fantasy, male prescriptions for us, estranged from our own experience because our education has not reflected or echoed it. I would suggest not biology, but ignorance of ourselves, has been the key to our powerlessness.

> (Rich 1985: 24)

With knowledge of ourselves, and each other, we might no longer be powerless, and I suspect that this is why we meet so much resistance to feminist ways of working. The education of women is a dangerous thing.

Acknowledgements

I should like to thank my colleagues on the New Opportunities for Women programme for their comments on the part of this chapter that describes work which belongs to all of us. I should also like to thank my teaching partners, Rosie Stacy and Beryl Whyatt, with whom much of my analysis has been and is being developed.

10

Emancipating Rita: the limits of change

Sue Gollop

Setting the scene

Apart from the two brief terms I spent at London University as an undergraduate before leaving to get married, I have combined my pursuit of higher education, both as a full-time and as a part-time student, with the roles of wife and mother. Because of this, in my current position as a lecturer in initial teacher education I have always felt a particular affinity for those mature women students who embark on a long course of study while continuing to maintain home and family. With the increased provision of access courses for mature students and with the decreasing number of school leavers, many institutions of higher education with little tradition of understanding and meeting the needs of mature students are being confronted by demands very different from those previously encountered with a largely school-leaver cohort of students. As tutor with special responsibility for first-year students, I saw an opportunity to explore, in the context of formal research, the process of change with a group of mature women in their first year of full-time study. I wanted to help sustain them in their new student roles and to further my own learning, both as a continuing student now engaged in a higher degree and to inform change within my institution. The purpose of this enquiry, then, was to investigate change as a personal process and to make use of that learning so that change might be effectively and creatively managed for both the researched and the researcher. Together we sought to understand the context of change by sharing histories and common concerns. We also explored the nature of change in terms of the competing demands it made on the lives of the women and their families. I feel that we need to know where we are coming from if we are to recognize the demands we make of ourselves and those others make of us, and if we are to accommodate, with minimal conflict, to the new demands that necessarily accompany change. For all these women, their multiple roles as students, wives and mothers were permeated with guilt at not always being 'able to cope':

> My main problem has been overcoming feelings of guilt at leaving my children more than I was used to.

> My husband has a silent way of making me feel guilty. He has a point. All this hassle is because of me. I am not able to cope.

One way of dealing with guilt is to understand its source and to recognize those structures which contrive to sustain it and a sense of inadequacy in the 'guilty'. The search for such an understanding increasingly came to underpin the whole enquiry: I wanted the research process itself to act as a catalyst for 'knowing reality in order to change it' (Lather 1986b: 272).

This chapter is concerned with the students' stories, but in particular with the story of one student, Rita, who compelled me to acknowledge the power and relevance of 'biography, personal relationships or social context' in what Salmon (1980: 6) sees as affecting 'both what people already know and the modes through which they are able to learn'. I wanted the process of research into change to help the students themselves to change and to grow as self-fulfilling individuals. Yet it was the students themselves who insisted I take account of their lives and their own interpretations of events.

The clipped-wing syndrome

In my work as a tutor working with third-year BEd students, I had previously carried out a small research project on student-led seminars. For one term, I had asked the students to take responsibility for organizing and leading an option course. I wanted to give the students real responsibility for their own learning, where they took turns in setting up the seminar room, providing input on a given theme, leading discussions and facilitating group tasks. They were also required to evaluate sessions in terms of their own learning and the quality of the learning experience. A transcript of a taped discussion between three student participants at the end of the course concluded like this:

> *Fay*:   At last we had the opportunity to do something for ourselves.
> *Julie*:   Yes, we don't really do much for ourselves as learners. We still expect to get it from the 'experts' and we forget we can be our own experts.
> *Fay*:   But do we really want to take that on? That responsibility?
> *Sophie*: I sometimes wonder.

Here is a group of third-year student-teachers, each with at least 16 years of formal education behind them, recognizing their ability to contribute to their own learning and yet at the same time questioning their willingness to take responsibility for it. Yet why was I surprised? Their educational biographies had perhaps conditioned and constrained these learners to the extent that they seemed hesitant about exploring alternative strategies for learning. Given this opportunity to organize their own learning, they felt not empowered but trapped by past experience of what they felt teaching and learning should properly be. I was reminded of the acid comment made by Simone de Beauvoir (1960: 336) about the blame attached to woman made impotent by man: 'Her wings are clipped and it's found deplorable she cannot fly.'

I began to look at my students in the light of their 'clipped wings' and the changes I had expected. Subsequent interviews and their written evaluations of each session revealed a range of reactions and responses to the term of student-led seminars. Not only could many not fly, but they did not appear to want to. Even worse, some did not even know they were supposed to. Undoubtedly a few of the student group made the most of their new-found freedom and soared. Some of them were prepared to venture forth tentatively with some support. The majority were confused by the experience and seemed to say, 'We don't need freedom, we're alright as we are'. They stayed where they were, grumbling and muttering about unnecessary disturbances.

The research design I had engaged in offered these students little help in managing the changes I was expecting of them. There was no opportunity for the participants to make use of the research data that we had gathered throughout the term in order to help themselves. There was none of what Lather (1986b: 263) calls 'reciprocity' in the research design, in which 'we consciously use our research to help participants understand and change their situations'. The research served my purposes not theirs.

It was at this stage that I was appointed to the role of year tutor with responsibility for first-year students. Two particular research concerns surfaced: I became increasingly interested in the management of change at a time when the education world in England and Wales was confronted with change on an unprecedented scale; and in the polytechnic the new intake of BEd students contained a sizeable group of mature students. I decided therefore to focus my own research on a group of 15 mature women with families and on their struggles to come to terms with a critical life-history change in their first year of becoming teachers. I was determined to learn from the barren research project on student-led seminars; in this next study the research process itself must address the concerns of the participants and further their understanding of what was happening to them. I needed then to find a methodology that gave participants a formative strategy for managing and taking control of change.

Emancipatory research as a strategy for managing change

Marris (1974: 12) claims that if conflict arising out of change is to be resolved then there is a need to 'work out an interpretation of oneself and the world which preserves, despite estrangement, the thread of meaning'. If we are unable to preserve this 'thread of meaning' in times of change, we become disoriented by what Marris (1974: 150) describes as 'loss of attachment' and overwhelmed by 'a self-destructive betrayal of the meaning of past experience'.

The model of change presented by Marris suggests that it is a personal process involving an act of cognition. To neglect the person within the change is to see the individual as passive and unable to shape events. When individuals are so perceived, argues Marris, change is a form of bereavement so that it is experienced as a deep sense of loss. This sense of loss promotes disempowerment, for the individual feels events are out of his or her control. Lather (1986b) urges us to use the research process to help participants understand their disempowerment as the first step to challenging its grip. This is what she describes as 'emancipatory' research, which is committed to empowering participants and which enables them to take charge of their lives. My dissatisfaction with the research project on student-led seminars had stemmed largely from the unreciprocated learning that the methodology promoted – what Foucault (1977) would call a 'surveillance' by the researcher of the researched – which served to sustain the 'wing-clipping' process described by de Beauvoir.

Accordingly, I sought to develop a catalytic mode of enquiry based on the work of Lather (1986b) and her description of a reciprocal research design. Lather draws on the ideas and concepts of critical theory, with its concern for emancipation, empowerment, justice and transformation. Critical theories, says Grundy (1987: 18), 'are theories about persons and society which explain how coercion and distortion operate to inhibit freedom'. Underlying them is an implicit proposition that the social order is unjust. The focus of this enquiry, a group of women, all with families, seeking career changes which would necessarily involve upheaval within their families, meant that conflict and struggle were possible. Although the changes might not involve what Marris (1974) terms 'a sense of loss' for the women, their families might feel such a loss and resist any disturbance, so the generation of guilt and anxiety was probable. This cluster of factors – conflict, struggle and anxiety arising out of change, experienced by a group of women who might support each other over a long period of time – is characteristic of feminist consciousness raising groups who seek enlightenment, empowerment and the goal of social emancipation. Such collaborative and democratic groups have enabled many women, says Fay (1977: 232), 'to gain the emotional strength to accept and act on one's new insights'. It is not surprising then that critical theory and the feminist movement have found a fruitful partnership: 'The feminist enterprise bears the hallmarks of critical theory. It identifies the social construction of gender, rendering '"natural" what is social' (Gibson 1986: 157). A research design with an explicit political engagement is about doing research in an unjust world; my research is about women and by women and like the work of Oakley (1981) and Purvis (1985) it calls for a more just landscape in which to unfold women's stories.

Introducing Rita

The focus of this chapter is Rita, who, early in the first term of the course, wryly described herself as being 'out on loan from the family.' Here was a woman who told her own story of felt injustice and who now sought to fulfil old ambitions in the face of considerable difficulties. When Rita began the BEd degree, she was 35 years old, married, with two children aged 9 and 11. Before starting the four-year course, she had completed a part-time diploma course in a college where her husband, already a qualified accountant, was a full-time student reading theology. After his degree, the family moved to London, where the husband started work with a missionary society and Rita started her teacher training. She shared many of her early experiences with me. She described her bitterness at not being able to stay on at school after her father's death:

> I always wanted to be a teacher. When I was 15 my father had a heart attack and so I had to leave school at 16 to get a job. My mother forced me to leave . . . . I got a job in an insurance company . . . . There was no future in it. Women were viewed as fodder for the offices. Boys were put into a training programme for management.

This account of an experience that had happened 20 years before suggested that Rita was clearly alive to the injustice of her position as a young girl in search of education and aware of the status of women in the economic structure. She also described her current struggles to cope with the demands of family, coursework and preparation for the first teaching practice: 'I find myself very emotional and living on my nerves.' But she concluded: 'It's not all difficult. It's good because I feel more myself than I ever did. Whether that's a good thing I'm not sure. Now I feel I'm myself – my own person – doing something I consider to be worthwhile.' Although she doubted whether it was a 'good thing' to feel more herself, she acknowledged her new-found sense of personal fulfilment – a sense, at least, of worth if not of contentment. Yet given the house move, the demands of her husband's new job and the children's initial difficulties in settling into their new life in London, early in the course she felt that her own decision to start the BEd degree course should have been postponed for at least a year. Nevertheless, she thought that she 'ought to be able to manage better; there were other students in much more difficult circumstances.' In June, just before the first-year examinations, she came to see me and told me she had decided to leave the course at the end of term. She summed up her problems as 'divided loyalties'. She talked about the children:

> The children needed time to adapt. I didn't have time for them to invite friends home . . . and I think you need to be there to pick them up from school. One of the boys (in the first term) was set on by a group of older lads and an Alsatian . . . . I felt as if it were my fault. If I'd been there it wouldn't have happened.

She described her husband's work: 'He suddenly found himself in a situation where he was away from home a lot, working long hours, most weekends – his career has always been the most important thing.' There were also demands made on the wives by the missionary society. They were considered as equal, though unwaged, members of the society, which had not been made explicit initially: 'When we came down for interview, they seemed completely interested in [my husband]. They were not interested in me at all.'

Over the Easter vacation, there was a conference of all the members, including the wives. Rita had just finished an exhausting first teaching practice and she now had some lengthy written course work to complete: 'I didn't actually go in the end. We took [my husband] up . . . . And that brought it to a head . . . I felt as if I was letting them all down. All the other wives were there and they'd done lots of cooking.' It was at this point that she made the final decision to leave:

> Decisions had to be made as to whether we could both carry on – both branching out in two completely different directions. I felt my commitment had to be to my family and to the work my husband is involved in. . . . My husband's work has become more intense and he felt he could no longer carry me. . . . I felt I had to make a choice between my commitment to teaching and my involvement with the society.

What had happened to her long-held ambition to be a teacher? What about her sense of injustice to women? What about her new found sense of personal worth? Tentatively, yet within the emancipatory mode of enquiry, I reminded her of this last point: 'You remember in your last interview, you said although you felt torn, you did at last feel your "own person"?' She replied, 'Yes I did and I still do. But that's got to go by the board. There's no resentment. It's about commitment. It was a joint decision . . . . I think I've learned a lot about myself – such as times when I can't cope.' We were almost back full circle to Rita's life of 20 years earlier, a surrender yet again of her ambition to be a teacher, confirmed in a sense of inadequacy, but this time with no apparent feeling of injustice and no real sense of loss. Fromm (1942) writes: 'The child starts with giving up the expression of his feeling and eventually gives up the very feeling itself.'

Is this what had happened to Rita? The wing-clipping process disempowers slowly but not necessarily painfully. Custom and what is seen as 'natural' contrive to anaesthetize the victim over time. As I listened to Rita, I felt increasingly unhappy about what seemed to me to be her collusion in her own defeat, about what Freire (1970) might recognize as the 'oppressor within the oppressed'. We concluded the discussion like this:

Rita: It fits in with my beliefs.
Me: Is it part of your Christian faith?
Rita: Oh yes . . . we looked for guidance.
Me: So is it the sort of decision you would pray about?
Rita: Oh yes inevitably, because it's part of what I would consider to be guidance in my life.

Who needs emancipation?

An emancipatory intent is no guarantee of an emancipatory outcome.
(Acker *et al.* 1983: 431)

This seemed to be the ideal scenario for testing the power of emancipatory research to challenge and transform, but when Rita made the final decision to leave I found no satisfactory way forward. Throughout the year we had shared and reflected on many areas of mutual concern. After Rita's announcement there was barely a month left of the academic year. There was little time to promote further inquiry, to re-evaluate, to challenge and to argue as I had intended within the emancipatory research paradigm, and, indeed, as I had done with the other women in the research group throughout the year. My inertia arose out of what I could only interpret as her total submission to what she saw as the will of God. It would have been easy to dismiss Rita's acceptance of divine guidance as false consciousness but the literature of critical social science is permeated with the history of tyrannies, where 'liberators' have sought to remove the distortions of false consciousness only to replace old oppressions with new ones. I was in fact unable to counter her claim that prayer confirmed her decision. What looked to me like exploitation – by the missionary society, by her husband, by her family – which meant the sacrifice of old ambition and of her new feelings of personal worth, was not exploitation in her understanding. For my part, an inability to understand the nature of unshakeable faith gave me no point of entry into her world. Emancipating Rita seemed no longer feasible and perhaps it was not even appropriate. Emancipation serves the oppressed, but where there is no sense of oppression there is no feeling of need for emancipation. Yet feminist studies are littered with case histories of women who are trapped by what Comstock (1982, cited in Lather 1986b) describes as 'ideologically frozen understandings' that serve the interests of the dispossessed so inadequately. To accept the world as it is will do nothing for the oppressed.

Liz – a comparative case study

> Practices are changed by changing the ways in which they are understood.
>   (Carr and Kemmis 1986: 91)

I sought to understand the impasse I had reached with Rita by reflecting on the data I had gathered over the year on other women in the group who were struggling to maintain their place on the course against seemingly overwhelming odds. Liz was in a similar family situation to Rita – married, with two young children. She had made several attempts to pursue higher education but her husband's opposition, ably supported by his mother, had led to intolerable strain within the family and Liz had abandoned her studies: 'In the past . . . I've given up but this time I'm determined. I've always given in to the way he wanted to do things . . . . I want to do something worth- while with my life – something for me, no longer only just being the boys' mother, my husband's wife, daddy's little girl.' She described a critical event in her life which she felt had enabled real change. Five years previously her husband had become seriously ill and Liz had taken over every aspect of family life: 'I had this great taste of freedom and it did change me.'

Towards the end of the first year of her course, her husband's opposition wavered but with the onset of the second year of the course his objections surfaced with renewed vigour and I wondered if Liz would have enough strength to cope with the multiple demands of competing worlds. She described her position like this: 'I now have more control over my own life. I don't feel guilty now – I did feel guilty all last year. Now I'm thinking differently. You've got to change your vision.'

We talked about 'thinking differently' and how this might describe learn- ing for change. We spent some time sharing life-histories, focusing on the gender and class issues that complicate and sustain women's dis- empowerment. The dominant theme throughout this study was the debili- tating guilt felt by all the women as they tried to juggle new and old roles while attempting to smother any shock waves before they should disturb the family routine. To feel guilty, particularly as a mother of young children, was acknowledged by these women to be the heaviest of burdens. Liz, in her first year, had to fight hard to gain insights that would help her to recognize those unjust structures that sustain guilt. At the end of the first year she was able to analyse what had enabled her to 'think differently':

1 The need for self-fulfilment and feeling that she had the right to seek it: 'I want to do something worthwhile with my life . . . . I don't feel guilty now.'
2 The sense of a last chance: 'A stronger feeling now is one of having a second chance – it might be the last.'
3 The long-held ambition to pursue higher education and a sense of in-equality related to class: 'My social class counted – there were no ex-pectations for me [at school].'
4 The impetus of a definite career goal: 'I know where I'm going.'
5 The felt need to have [future] earning power.
6 The past experience of being able to cope during her husband's illness.
7 The taste of freedom enjoyed in coping at that time.
8 The habit of battling in the face of opposition: 'Support from home seems very important. On the other hand my lack of support made me more determined . . . . I've always been a rebel . . . if not very effective.'
9 A determination not to repeat her mother's existence: 'She was totally trampled on.'
10 Diminished guilt feelings arising from role conflicts, achieved particu-larly by talking to the other mature women students in the research group with similar concerns.

Liz's unwillingness to accept disempowerment gave her the impetus to do battle in an unjust world. Structures which had sought to bend or break her will were recognized for what they were. Her belief in self was strong, whether innate or honed by experience. She held her family dear, as did all the students in the research group, but no longer would its concerns define her total existence: 'not', she said, 'to the exclusion of me.' She was well able to understand her past and present so that this learning could help transform her future. She used her own story as the springboard for change and stepped out of a biography which had trapped her. Carr (1987: 29) says that critical theory 'insists that the more individuals understand about the social determinants of their action the more likely they are to escape from the constraints.' Liz engaged in this reflective process in order to manage her own change.

Learning for change, however, will almost certainly involve those whose interests are best served by the existing order. Liz was sustained in her new student life by her own thinking about self and about where she, and those around her, came from. She was able to challenge and confront, if not deconstruct, those ideologies which disempowered so that she could, at least, 'think differently'. Yet in spite of her best efforts, Liz is still in the front line of the battle; she has learned about the nature of change but she must fight unless and until she can shift the perspectives of others who count in her life.

Interpreting reality

How do we explain the lives of others without violating their reality?
(Acker *et al.* 1983: 429)

So what about Rita? Like Liz, she seemed hedged about on all sides by constraints. She had engaged in rigorous analysis of her past, yet she made no connections from past to present to future as Liz was able to do. The kind of dialogue I was able to engage in with Liz at times of crisis did not seem appropriate when Rita came with her decision to leave. Within the group and with Rita individually, I had discussed feminist issues of women and education, expectations, equality and choice, but at no stage did religion enter our talk. For Rita, I now recognize, this was a glaring omission given the fundamental organizing force her faith so obviously was for her. However willing I might be to interpret her religious beliefs as part of a systematic wing-clipping process, I felt unable and unwilling to challenge openly what was for her one of 'the things people cling to because they provide direction and meaning in their lives' (Fay 1977: 214).

The unbroken 'thread of meaning' in Rita's life was located in her religion. Here she found comfort and support when all else – children, husband, family and college life – made demands on her that seemed overwhelmingly onerous and were perceived, by her and significant others in her life, to be largely problems of her own making. Managing change for Rita meant keeping disturbance at home to a minimum. Change arising from her new student role, which demanded complementary change in how her family thought about her, was never able, or perhaps never allowed by Rita, to impinge on other people's lives. Change which promotes a new set of values can only come about when the dominant and prevailing culture concedes space. Such change, says Holly (1987: 133), is so far-reaching as to be transforming since it involves critical events which 'cannot be assimilated until the structure accommodates'.

Many of the women saw change simply as a bolt-on package. Sophie, who like Rita left the course at the end of the first year, wrote: 'My husband is adjusting but he does get angry at times . . . . He does like the idea of me there cooking the meals. I'm the back-up system. I'm still trying to keep everything going.' This strategy worked at first until times of crises – sick children, cars that broke down – or until exhaustion began to set in.

For others there was a despairing acceptance of lengthy struggle ahead, to be endured with the help of the other women students: 'I don't expect anything will get better for me at home. Everybody's against me doing this [course] and since it was my choice to do it I can't really expect much. I will get there in spite of them all – with the support of the other matures around me.'

Some of the students were able and willing to resolve conflict by reflecting on their situations and challenging the values and practices in others that imposed limits on new aspirations:

> I know I can't do what I used to do for them [the family]. It would mean spreading myself so thinly in all directions. So my change has had to become their change even though they don't like it . . . . I feel I have been able to think more clearly about myself since I came to college. Old roles are not all-consuming . . . . I have given myself low priority in the past.

As a framework for analysis, I found useful the concept of the 'critical phase' described by Woods (1987: 62) as a period of choice, decision and change which 'project an individual in a different direction'. When at the end of the research I re-presented to the students, for validation (they had insisted on alterations first), a final hypothesis about the nature of the critical phase in the change process that I called 'transformation', I described it like this:

> As wives and/or mothers, you all have special responsibilities you have to and/or want to fulfil. However, by recognizing your own need for personal fulfilment and by claiming it as your right, you are empowered to take on new and additional roles without a sense of guilt. This does not mean you neglect old roles but
>
> 1 You are able to think about them differently.
> 2 You help others to think differently about you.
> 3 You are able to think before and beyond the immediate present.

Few if any of the students felt they had reached this phase at the end of their first year. They had learned something about the nature of change and its limits in terms of individual endeavour. Change as an act of cognition was confirmed for me through this research; that it is not enough for individuals to want to seek change for themselves was also powerfully confirmed. Although personal change enables us to understand and challenge reality, we can only do something about that reality when change operates beyond the level of the individual. The limits imposed by individual change contributed to Liz's dilemma and to Rita's departure.

The limits of emancipatory enquiry and critical theory

Humans are not only active beings but they are also embodied, traditional, historical and embedded creatures . . . and their will to change is circumscribed in all sorts of ways.

(Fay 1987: 9)

A research methodology drawing on critical theory had little if anything to say to Rita, and left Liz where she wanted to be on the course, but still struggling and 'circumscribed in all sorts of ways'. So what has critical theory to learn from women like Rita and Liz? Fay (1987) reminds us that, as human beings, we are bound by the body, caught up in tradition, shaped through history and dependent on each other in an intricate set of relationships. All the women in the study sought change, but they experienced it in different ways at different times – as loss, as renewal, as revitalization, as reorientation. Yet it always gave rise to anxiety, most often manifested and defined as guilt. As part of the research process we tried to control anxiety by recognizing that:

1 Anxiety is always part of the change process.
2 Anxiety feeds on dark corners of thinking and practice which seek to maintain old ways.
3 We can understand and confront anxiety by illuminating and examining those dark corners.
4 This confrontation is enabled within a supportive group.

As well as confronting anxiety, these women were always conscious of looking at their own change within the context of the needs and history of the family. Rightly they insisted that I should not overlook or dismiss these concerns. However, those who felt they should be able and ought to cope were not necessarily best equipped to do so, since they did not always recognize how both the surrounding structures in which they were embedded and the thinking, practices and demands of others disabled or constrained the process of change that they were seeking. Rita was perhaps in this situation. Those who recognized and understood their own disempowerment were better able to cope with the guilt and anxiety which arose out of change taking place within the context of family life. Although to understand was not necessarily to be able to change, it did help to sustain the individual's struggle: 'I'm still left with all the ironing and the housework but if it doesn't get done, too bad. I've got new horizons and I feel good.' This is not emancipation but, as Liz found, it is a considerable step on the way towards it.

Change was most actively managed where it was seen as a collaborative enterprise, over time, within the whole family, and when it was underpinned by a clear understanding that reality is socially constructed. One student described her situation like this:

Prior to starting the course, we made a point that we did the housework together at the weekend . . . then the children took this democratic vote they didn't want school dinners . . . . Now the 7- and
9-year-olds butter the bread and the youngest gets the fruit and we do
it together – and my husband. I consciously stand back . . . I look at
my husband – everything done for him as a child. But I was, from the
age of 9, brought up just by my mother. My mother's attitude was
'Don't let anybody down-tread you.' . . . But I wouldn't like to go
through that first year of marriage again, it was horrendous. Now I
don't feel guilt-ridden if it goes wrong – that it's my fault. It's a sharing
of lives – a cooperative venture.

Undoubtedly some students were embedded in wider and more complex
relationships than others. The mother–child network exerted a powerful
influence for all the women in the group. But they also gave accounts of
themselves as sisters, daughters, daughters-in-law, wives and ex-wives: all
these roles helped define, determine and influence practice and view of
self, and in particular the potential for change. Those without husbands
agreed they were able to take on the student role with greater ease. The
paradox of the husband, described by one student as 'someone to offer
comfort and to support, and yet in the same breath to demand', found
general agreement.

Given the fragile and untidy nature of human existence, there can be little
doubt that change, whether sought or imposed, is better managed as a
'cooperative venture', if only in recognition of the interrelatedness of all
human enterprise. Although we often have little control over the countless
factors which impinge on our lives, to understand how they help to define
us is to begin to question and perhaps to recognize that alternatives exist.
The changing perspectives of these mature women students did not always
synchronize with the views and beliefs of those around around them and
this gave rise to dissonance. For some this was unacceptable and they
retreated to old ground. But others found the strength to endure this
dissonance, through group support, through learning to think and feel
differently about themselves, but perhaps more significantly by helping to
shift the perspectives of others who counted in their lives. 'Liberatory
learning', say Freire and Shor (1987: 101), 'is a social activity' and cannot be
conceived in individual terms.

Conclusion

To change our own thinking about self is a crucial first step, if the change
we seek is liberatory in intent and outcome. It involves challenging power
structures through an understanding of where we are and how we have come
to be located within those structures. Yet change in self-understanding can

never be enough if what we seek is not to be distorted or denied by the ideologies of others. Furthermore, our lives are intricately bound together in a web of relationships, rooted in history and tradition, that both constrain and sustain us so that any effective change, and particularly liberatory change with its search for social justice, must reverberate beyond the individual. Such change is therefore best conceived and worked for as a cooperative human enterprise. This approach acknowledges the interrelatedness of human existence and might help, as one student said in trying to establish within her family new patterns of thinking and practice arising from her student role, in 'looking for a more equal future [rather] than resenting an unequal past'.

References

Abercrombie, M. L. J. (1969). *The Anatomy of Judgement: an Investigation into the Processes of Perception and Reason*, Harmondsworth: Penguin.

Acker, J., Barry, K. and Esseveld, J. (1983). 'Objectivity and truth: problems in doing feminist research', *Women's Studies International Forum* 6, 4: 423–35.

Acker, S. (ed.) (1984). *Women and Education: World Yearbook of Education*, London: Kogan Page.

Aird, E. (1985). *From a Different Perspective: Change in Women's Education*, London: Workers' Educational Association.

Aird, E. (1986). 'Gender, education and change'. In D. Punter (ed.) *Introduction to Contemporary Cultural Studies*, Harlow: Longman.

Argyris, C. and Schon, D. (1974). *Theory in Practice: Increasing Professional Effectiveness*, San Francisco: Jossey-Bass.

Ashcroft, K. (1987). 'The history of an innovation', *Assessment and Evaluation in Higher Education* 12: 37–45.

Ashcroft, K. and Griffiths, M. (1989). 'Reflective teachers and reflective tutors; school experience in an initial teacher education course', *Journal of Education for Teaching* 15: 35–52.

Ashcroft, K. and Tann, S. (1988). 'Beyond building better checklists; staff development in a school experience programme', *Assessment and Evaluation in Higher Education* 13: 61–72.

Barnes, D. and Todd, F. (1977). *Communication and Learning in Small Groups*, London: Routledge and Kegan Paul.

Bartky, S. L. (1975). 'Toward a phenomenology of feminist consciousness', *Social Theory and Practice* 3, 4: 425–39.

Bezucha, R. J. (1985). 'Feminist pedagogy as a subversive activity'. In M. Culley and C. Partuges (eds) *Gendered Subjects: the Dynamics of Feminist Teaching*, London: Routledge and Kegan Paul.

Biott, C. (1991). *Semi-Detached Teachers: Building Advisory and Support Relationships in Classrooms*, London: Falmer Press.

Biott, C., Taylor, C., Errington, B. and Grice, G. (1989). *Professional Development and INSET Opportunities: a Study in Six Primary Schools*, South Tyneside LEA (mimeo).

Bird, T. and Little, J. W. (1986). 'How schools organize the teaching occupation', *Elementary School Journal* 86, 4: 493–511.

Bolam, R. (1984). 'Recent research on the dissemination and implementation of educational innovations'. In G. Campbell (ed.) *Health Education and Youth: a Review of Research and Developments*, London: Falmer.

Bolam, R. (1986). 'School improvement: the national scene', *School Organisation* 6, 3: 314–20.

Bredo, A. E. and Bredo, E. R. (1975). 'Effects of environment and structure on the process of innovation'. In J. V. Baldridge and T. E. Deal (eds) *Managing Change in Educational Organisations*, Berkeley, Calif.: McCutcheon.

Brown, S., McIntyre, D. and McAlpine, A. (1988). 'The knowledge which underpins the craft of teaching', American Educational Research Association, Annual Conference, New Orleans.

Bunch, C. and Pollack, S. (eds) (1983). *Learning Our Way: Essays in Feminist Education*, Trumansburg, NY: Crossing Press.

CACE (1967). *Children and Their Primary Schools*, Plowden Report, London: HMSO.

Campbell, P. A. (1987). 'School Development Plans', a report prepared for Suffolk Education Authority and the Cambridge Institute of Education (mimeo).

Campbell, P. A. (1989). 'Year of transition: a study of school development', unpublished MA Dissertation, University of East Anglia.

Campbell, R. J. (1985). *Developing the Primary School Curriculum*, London: Cassell.

Carr, W. (1987). 'Critical theory and educational studies', *Journal of Philosophy of Education* 21, 2: 287–95.

Carr, W. and Kemmis, S. (1986). *Becoming Critical: Education, Knowledge and Action Research*, London: Falmer Press.

Christensen, J., Burke, P. and Fessler, R. (1983). 'Teacher life-span development: a summary and synthesis of the literature', paper presented at the Annual Meeting of the American Educational Research Association, Montreal.

Clegg, A. (1980). *About Our Schools*, Oxford: Basil Blackwell.

Culley, M. and Portuges, C. (eds) (1985). *Gendered Subjects: the Dynamics of Feminist Teaching*, London: Routledge and Kegan Paul.

Dalin, P. (1978). *Limits to Educational Change*, London: Macmillan.

Davis, B. H. (1983). 'Teaching the feminist minority'. In C. Bunch and S. Pollack (eds) *Learning Our Way*, Trumansburg, NY: Crossing Press.

Day, C. (1987). 'Professional learning through collaborative inservice activity'. In W. J. Smyth (ed.) *Educating Teachers: Changing the Nature of Pedagogical Knowledge*, London: Falmer Press.

Day, C. (1989). 'Issues in the management of appraisal for professional development', *Westminster Studies in Education* 12: 3–15.

De Beauvoir, S. (1960). *The Second Sex*, translated H. M. Parshley, Harmondsworth: Penguin.

DES (1989a). *Initial Teacher Training: Approval of Courses*, Circular 24/89, 10 November.

DES (1989b). *The Implementation of the Local Authority Training Grant Scheme (LEATGS): Report on the First Year of the Scheme*, London: HMSO.

Desforges, C. and McNamara, D. (1979). 'Theory and practice: methodological procedures for the objectification of craft knowledge', *British Journal of Teacher Education* 5: 145–52.

Du Bois, B. (1983). 'Passionate scholarship: notes on values, knowing and method in feminist social science'. In G. Bowles and R. D. Klein (eds) *Theories of Women's Studies*, London: Routledge and Kegan Paul.

Dubois, E. C. *et al.* (1985). *Feminist Scholarship: Kindling in the Groves of Academe*, Champaign: University of Illinois Press.

Easen, P. (1991). 'The visible supporter with no visible means of support: the ESG teacher and the classteacher'. In C. Biott (ed.) *Semi-Detached Teachers*, London: Falmer Press.

Eichler, M. (1980). *The Double Standard: a Feminist Critique of Social Science*, London: Croom Helm.

Eichler, M. (1988). *Nonsexist Research Methods: a Practical Guide*, London: Allen and Unwin.

Eisenstein, H. (1984). *Contemporary Feminist Thought*, London: Unwin.

Elliott, J. (1976). 'Developing hypotheses about classrooms from teachers' practical constructs: an account of the work of the Ford Teaching Project', *Interchange* 7, 2: 2–21.

Elliott J. (1981). 'Action research; framework for self evaluation in schools', TIQL working paper No. 1, Cambridge Institute of Education (mimeo).

Elliott, J. (1987). 'Educational theory, practical philosophy and action research', *British Journal of Educational Studies* 35: 2.

Fay, B. (1977). 'How people change themselves: the relationship between critical theory and its audience'. In T. Ball (ed.) *Political Theory and Praxis*, Minneapolis: University of Minnesota Press.

Fay, B. (1987). *Critical Social Science: Liberation and Its Limits*, Cambridge: Polity Press.

Foucault, M. (1977). *Discipline and Punish: Birth of the Prison*, London: Allen Lane.

Freire, P. (1970). *Pedagogy of the Oppressed*, New York: Herder and Herder.

Freire, P. and Shor, I. (1987). *A Pedagogy for Liberation*, London: Macmillan.

Fromm, E. (1942). *Fear of Freedom*, London: Routledge.

Fullan, M. (1982). *The Meaning of Educational Change*, Columbia, NY: Teachers' College Press.

Fullan, M. (1986). 'Improving the implementation of educational change', *School Organisation* 6, 3: 321–6.

Fullan, M. (1991). *The New Meaning of Educational Change*, London: Cassell.

Gearhart, A. M. (1983). 'If the mortarboard fits . . . radical feminism in academia'. In C. Bunch and S. Pollack (eds) *Learning Our Way*, Trumansburg, NY: Crossing Press.

Gibson, R. (1986). *Critical Theory and Education*, London: Hodder and Stoughton.

Gillman, C. (1990). 'Classroom strategies: an exercise in collaboration between pairs of teachers in a mainstream school', unpublished MA thesis, Newcastle upon Tyne Polytechnic.

Glaser, B. C. and Strauss, A. L. (1976). *The Discovery of Grounded Theory: Strategies for Qualitative Research*, New York: Aldine.

Grundy, S. (1987). *From Curriculum to Praxis*, London: Falmer Press.

Hall, G. E. and Loucks, S. (1978). 'Teacher concerns as a basis for facilitating and personalizing staff development', *Teachers' College Record* 80, September: 36–53.

Hargreaves, A. (1990). 'Contrived collegiality: a sociological analysis', International Sociological Association Conference, Madrid.

Harland, J. (1990). *The Work and Impact of Advisory Teachers*, Slough: NFER.

Hartley, D. (1985). *Understanding the Primary School: a Sociological Analysis*, London: Croom Helm.

Hogben, D. and Lawson, M. J. (1984). 'Trainee and beginning teacher attitude stability and change: four case studies', *Educational Research* 21: 212–21.

Holly, P. (1987). *Action Research: Cul-de-sac or Turnpike?*, Cambridge: Cambridge Institute of Education (mimeo).

Holt, J. (1969). *How Children Fail*, Harmondsworth: Penguin.

Howe, F. (1983). 'Feminist scholarship: the extent of the revolution'. In C. Bunch and S. Pollack (eds) *Learning our Way*, Trumansburg, NY: Crossing Press.

Hughes, M. and Kennedy, M. (1985). *New Futures: Changing Women's Education*, London: Routledge and Kegan Paul.

ILEA (1986). *The Junior Schools Project*, London: ILEA.

Isaac, J. and Ashcroft, K. (1987). 'A leap into the practical'. In *Enquiring Teachers, Further Concerns*, Cambridge: Cambridge Institute of Education (mimeo).

Klein, R. D. (1984). 'Women's studies: the challenge to man-made education'. In S. Acker (ed.) *Women and Education*, London: Kogan Page.

Klein, R. D. (1987). 'The dynamics of the women's studies classroom: review essay', *Women's Studies International Forum* 10, 2: 187–206.

Kuhn, T. S. (1970). *The Structure of Scientific Revolution*, Chicago: Chicago University Press.

Lather, P. (1984). 'Critical theory, curricular transformation and feminist mainstreaming', *Journal of Education* 166: 49–62.

Lather, P. (1986a). 'Issues of validity in openly ideological research: between a rock and a soft place', *Interchange* 17, 4: 63–84.

Lather, P. (1986b). 'Research as praxis', *Harvard Educational Review* 56, 3: 257–77.

Lewis, C. S. (1968). *Voyage to Venus*, London: Pan Books.

Little, J. W. (1988). 'Assessing the prospects for teacher leadership'. In A. Lieberman (ed.) *Building a Professional Culture in Schools*, Columbia, NY: Teachers College Press.

Mahony, P. (1988). 'Oppressive pedagogy: the importance of process in women's studies', *Women's Studies International Forum* 11, 2: 103–8.

Marquand, D. (1988). *The Unprincipled Society: New Demands and Old Politics*, London: Fontana.

Marris, P. (1974). *Loss and Change*, London: Routledge.

McNeil, L. (1988). 'Contradictions of control, part 1: administrators and teachers', *Phi Delta Kappa* January: 333–9.

McNiff, J. (1988). 'Action research: a generative model for in-service support', *British Journal of In-Service Education* Summer: 40–66.

Mezirow, J. A. (1981). 'A practical theory of adult learning and education', *Adult Education* 31, 1: 3–24.

Mies, M. (1983). 'Towards a methodology for feminist research'. In G. Bowles and R. D. Klein (eds) *Theories of Womens' Studies*, London: Routledge and Kegan Paul.

Nias, J. (1986). 'Reference groups in primary teaching'. In S. J. Ball and I. F. Goodson (eds) *Teachers' Lives and Careers*, London: Falmer Press.

Nias, J. (1987). *Seeing Anew: Teachers' Theories of Action*, Geelong, Victoria: Deakin University Press.

Nias, J. (1989). *Primary Teachers Talking: a Study of Teaching as Work*, London: Routledge.

Nias, J. (1991). 'Changing times, changing identities: grieving for a lost self'. In R. Burgess (ed.) *Educational Research and Evaluation*, London: Falmer Press.

Nias, J., Southworth, G. and Campbell, P. (1992). *Whole School Development in the Primary School*, London: Falmer Press.

Nias, J., Southworth, G. and Yeomans, R. (1989). *Primary School Staff Relationships: a Study of Organisational Cultures*, London: Cassell.

Oakley, A. (1981). 'Interviewing women: a contradiction in terms'. In H. Roberts (ed.) *Doing Feminist Research*, Boston: Routledge and Kegan Paul.

Peters, R. S. (1970). *Ethics and Education*, London: Allen and Unwin.

Piaget, J. (1958). *The Development of Logical Thinking from Childhood to Adolescence*, London: Routledge.

Piaget, J. (1969). *The Mechanics of Perception*, translated by G. N. Seagrim, London: Routledge.

Piaget, J. (1972). *Psychology and Epistemology*, Harmondsworth: Penguin.

Pollard, A. (1985). *The Social World of the Primary School*, London: Cassell.

Polyani, M. (1972). *Personal Knowledge*, Chicago: University of Chicago Press.

Popper, K. R. (1966). *The Open Society and Its Enemies*, London: Routledge.

Purvis, J. (1985). 'Historical documentary research from a feminist perspective'. In R. G. Burgess (ed.) *Strategies in Educational Research: Qualitative Methods*, London: Falmer Press.

Rich, A. (1985). 'Taking women students seriously'. In M. Culley and C. Portuges (eds) *Gendered Subjects: the Dynamics of Feminist Teaching*, London: Routledge and Kegan Paul.

Roberts, H. (1981). *Doing Feminist Research*, London: Routledge and Kegan Paul.

Roethke, T. (1968). *The Collected Poems*, London: Faber and Faber.

Rogers, C. (1961). *On Becoming a Person*, Boston: Houghton Mifflin.

Rogers, C. (1983). *Freedom to Learn for the 80s*, Columbus, Ohio: Charles E. Merrill.

Rorty, R. (1989). *Contingency, Irony and Solidarity*, Cambridge: Cambridge University Press.

Rowbotham, S. (1977). *Hidden from History*, London: Pluto.

Rudduck, J. and Hopkins, D. (1985). *Research as a Basis for Teaching*, London: Heinemann Educational.

Russell, T. (1988). 'From pre-service teacher education to first year of teaching: a story of theory and practice'. In J. Calderhead (ed.) *Teachers' Professional Learning*, London: Falmer Press.

Rutenberg, T. (1983). 'Learning women's studies'. In G. Bowles and R. D. Klein (eds) *Theories of Women's Studies*, London: Routledge and Kegan Paul.

Rutledge, D. (1988). 'Institutionalizing change: the problem of system beliefs'. In M. Lightfoot and N. Martin (eds) in association with the National Association for the Teaching of English, *The Word for Teaching Is Learning: Essays for James Britton*, London: Heinemann Educational.

Salmon, P. (ed.) (1980). *Coming to Know*, London: Routledge.

Schniedewind, N. (1983). 'Feminist values: guidelines for teaching methodology in women's studies'. In C. Bunch and S. Pollack (eds) *Learning Our Way*, Trumansburg, NY: Crossing Press.

Schon, D. (1983). *The Reflective Practitioner*, New York: Basic Books.

Schon, D. (1987). *Educating the Reflective Practitioner*, San Francisco, Calif.: Jossey Bass.

Schulman, L. (1984). 'Psychology and the limitations of individual rationality', *Review of Educational Research* 154, 4: 501–24.

Schulman, L. S. (1987). 'Knowledge and teaching: foundations of the new reform', *Harvard Educational Review* 57, 1: 1–22.

Showalter, E. (1978). *British Women Novelists from Brontë to Lessing*, London: Virago.

Simon, H. A. (1965). *Administrative Behaviour*, London: Collier Macmillan.

Smith, D. E. (1987). *The Everyday World as Problematic: a Feminist Sociology*, Oxford: Oxford University Press.

Somekh, B. (1991). 'Collaborative action research: working together towards professional development'. In C. Biott (ed.) *Semi-Detached Teachers*, London: Falmer Press.

Spender, D. (1983). *Women of Ideas and What Men Have Done to Them*, London: Routledge and Kegan Paul.

Stanley, L. and Wise, S. (1983). *Breaking Out: Feminist Consciousness and Feminist Research*, London: Routledge and Kegan Paul.

Sullivan, M. (1991). 'Working and learning in other people's classrooms'. In C. Biott (ed.) *Semi-Detached Teachers*, London: Falmer Press.

Taking Liberties Collective (1989). *Learning the Hard Way: Women's Oppression in Men's Education*, London: Macmillan.

Tallantyre, F. (1985). *Women at the Crossroads: Ten Years of New Opportunities for Women Courses in the Northern District*, London: Workers' Educational Association.

Vetterling-Braggin, M. *et al.* (1977). *Feminism and Philosophy*, Lanham, Md.: Littlefield and Adams.

Vygotsky, L. S. (1978). *Mind in Society*, Harvard: Harvard University Press.

Wagner, A. C. (1987). 'Knots in teachers' thinking'. In J. Calderhead (ed.) *Exploring Teachers' Thinking*, London: Cassell.

Walker, R. (1985). *Doing Research: a Handbook for Teachers*, London: Methuen.

Westkott, M. (1983). 'Women's studies as a strategy for change: between criticism and vision'. In G. Bowles and R. D. Klein (eds) *Theories of Women's Studies*, London: Routledge and Kegan Paul.

Whitehead, J. and Foster, D. (1984). *Action Research and Professional Development*, Classroom Action Research Bulletin, No. 6, Cambridge: Cambridge Institute of Education.

Wilson, S. M., Schulman, L. S. and Richert, A. E. (1987). '150 ways of knowing'. In J. Calderhead (ed.) *Exploring Teachers' Thinking*, London: Cassell.

Wolcott, H. (1977). *Teachers Versus Technocrats: an Educational Innovation in Anthropological Perspective*, Eugene, OR: Center for Educational Policy and Management, University of Oregon.

Wolverton, T. (1983). 'Unlearning complicity, remembering resistance: White women's anti-racism education'. In C. Bunch and S. Pollack (eds) *Learning Our Way*, Trumansburg, NY: Crossing Press.

Woods, P. (1987). 'Life-histories and teacher knowledge'. In W. J. Smyth (ed.) *Educating Teachers: Changing the Nature of Pedagogical Knowledge*, London: Falmer Press.

Woods, P. (1991). *Teacher Skills and Strategies*, London: Falmer Press.

Yeomans, R. (1987). 'Leading the team, belonging to the group'. In G. Southworth (ed.) *Readings in Primary School Management*, London: Falmer.

Zeichner, K. M., Tabachnick, R. B. and Densmore, K. (1987). 'Individual, institutional and cultural influences on the development of teachers' craft knowledge'. In J. Calderhead (ed.) *Exploring Teachers' Thinking*, London: Cassell.

Zeichner, K. M. and Teitelbaum, K. (1982). 'Personalised and inquiry-orientated teacher education: an analysis of two approaches to the development of curriculum for field-based experiences', *Journal of Education for Teaching* 8: 95–117.

Index

Abercrombie, M. L. J., xvi, 25
About Our Schools (Clegg), 69, 76–7
Acker, J., 139
Acker, S., 118–19, 127
action research, xv, 13, 65, 78, 89
  classic model, 36–7, 40
adult education, xiii, 109–29
advisory teachers, xii, xiii, xv, 3–4,
  64–5
  classroom credibility, 6, 87
  expectations of, 12, 87, 88
  relationship with class teachers,
    4–18, 87–9
  role, 4, 86, 90
  strategies of support, 12–14, 16, 17
advisory teaching, 3–18
affectivity, 21, 24–5, 27
Aird, E., 111, 123
anxiety, 67, 133, 141
apprenticeship model of teacher
  education, 33, 35, 38, 44
Argyris, C., 34–5
Ashcroft, K., 41, 42
assessment, 41–3, 127
attitudes, 8, 20
  shared, 21, 54
audiotape transcripts, 36, 97, 100

authoritarianism, 56, 68–9
authority in schools, 51, 56, 67, 68

Barnes, D., 97
Bartky, S. L., 117, 123
Beauvoir, S. de *see* de Beauvoir, S.
Bedford College of Higher Education,
  23, 24
beliefs, 20, 52, 67
  Christian, 51, 136, 139
  shared, 61, 104
Bezucha, R. J., 120
Biott, C., 4, 8, 87
Bird, T., 52
Bois, B. du *see* du Bois, B.
Bolam, R., 56
Bredo, A. E., 7
Bredo, E. R., 7
Brown, S., 15
Bunch, C., 114, 119–20

CACE, 19
California Mentor Teacher Program,
  6
Campbell, P. A., 49, 50, 53, 56
Campbell, R. J., 56
Carr, W., 34, 65, 137, 138

CATE, 44
change, personal, xv, 84, 90, 118
    management of, 132–4, 139–40
Christensen, J., 56
class teachers, 10, 39–40, 41
classroom experience, 91–106
classroom practice, 69–75, 80, 91–2,
    94–5, 103
classroom survival, 22
Clegg, A., 69, 76–7
consciousness raising, xiii, xvi, 115,
    116, 118, 122, 126, 133
    definition, 117
'contrived collegiality', 9–10
control, xvii, xx, 10, 69, 95
    see also discipline
'coping' in the classroom, 34–5
Council for the Accreditation of
    Teacher Education, 44
critical enquiry, xiv, xv, xxi, 34,
    36–8, 41–2, 44
'critical friendships', 13–14
critical theory, xv, xvi, 133–4, 141–2
Culley, M., 123
cultures, 27
    collaborative, 9, 30, 31
    courses, 23
    schools, xviii–xix, 15, 25, 30, 52,
        53–4
    staff, 9–10, 20–21, 30, 31
curriculum change, 21, 62, 80, 88
curriculum coordinators, 21, 24, 29
curriculum negotiation, 121–2

Dalin, P., 64
data collection 36–7, 40, 74
    see also audiotape transcripts;
        diaries; discussion sheets;
        interviews; observation
Davis, B. H., 123, 125, 127
Day, C., 13–14, 106
De Beauvoir, S., 128, 132, 133
deliberation, 33–4
Department of Education and Science,
    4, 44
deputy headteachers, xiii, xix
    partnerships with headteachers,
        49–61

DES, 4, 44
Desforges, C., 15
development partnerships, 11, 13,
    17–18
diaries, as data collection technique,
    69–72
didacticism, xvii, 53, 68, 95
discipline, xix, 51, 52, 55, 59, 60
    see also control
disempowerment, 133, 138–9, 141
    see also empowerment
Du Bois, B., 124
Dubois, E. C., 121

Easen, P., 12–13, 14
Education Reform Act (1988), xvii, 20,
    31, 78
Educational Support Grant Project, 5
educational theory, 34–5, 63, 69
Eichler, M., 127
Eisenstein, H., 117
Elliott, J., xvi, 65
emancipation, 137, 141
emotion in the classroom, xviii, 122–4
empowerment, 115, 133
    see also disempowerment
entitlements, 58
evaluation, as a research process, 36,
    65, 131
    see also self-evaluation
experience as a basis for knowledge,
    xviii, 63–4, 117
experiential learning, 28, 32, 36, 116

Fay, B., 133, 139, 141
feminism, xiii, xv, xvi, xviii, 121, 126,
    133–4
    see also women
Foster, D., 65
Foucault, M., 133
Freire, P., 136, 142
friendship, 79, 83, 84
    critical, 13–14
Fromm, E., 136
Fullan, M., xvi, 56, 64

Gearhart, A. M., 122
Gibson, R., 134

Gillman, C., 10–11
Glaser, B. C., 63
Gramsci, A., 118
Griffiths, M., 41
group membership, 27, 29, 43, 83
groups
   of student teachers, 24–30, 38–9,
      41–4
   of students, 96–7, 99–101
   of teachers, xviii, 57–9, 64–5, 69,
      79–85, 88–9
   of women, xviii, 79, 81, 113–14
   see also pairs; peer groups
Grundy, S., 133
guilt, xvi, 131, 133, 137–8, 140, 141

Hall, G. E., 56
Hargreaves, A., 9–10, 11
Harland, J., 12, 13, 16, 18
Hartley, D., 20
Hawthorn, N., 86
headteachers, xxii, xvii, xix, 21, 62–78
   partnerships with deputy
      headteachers, xix, 49–61
HMI, 4, 66
Hogben, D., 34
Holly, P., 139
Holt, J., 67
Hopkins, D., 65, 78
Howe, F., 118
Hughes, M., 114, 119, 120

ILEA, 19
implementation partnerships, 11, 13,
   14, 17–18
imposed support, 3, 4–11
INSET, 38, 39, 44, 89
   courses, 53, 58
interviews, as data collection
   technique, 49, 99–101, 105
Isaac, J., 42

Kemmis, S., 34, 65, 137
Kennedy, M., 114, 119, 120
Klein, R. D., 114–15, 116, 118, 119
knowledge, 63–4, 84
   professional, xv, 14–16, 17
Kuhn, T. S., 64

Lather, P., 110, 118, 127, 131, 132,
   133, 137
Lawson, M. J., 34
leadership, 6, 9, 21, 27
   by peers, 21, 28, 31
Learning Our Way (Bunch and
   Pollack), 114, 119–20
Learning the Hard Way (Taking
   Liberties Collective), 116, 120
Lewis, C. S., 61
licensed teacher scheme, 33, 38
Little, J. W., 6, 52
local management of schools, xxi, 39
Loucks, S., 56

McNamara, D., 15
McNeil, L., 6
McNiff, J., 65
Mahony, P., 115, 118
Marquand, D., 84
Marris, D., 133
men's role in women's studies,
   119–20
Mezirow, J. A., xvi, xix, 13, 17
Mies, M., 127

National Curriculum, xxi, 20, 21, 44,
   78, 82, 91
   in primary schools, 15, 16, 82
National Writing Project, xiii
   in Bedfordshire, 79–83, 87
   in Newcastle upon Tyne, 88
New Futures: Changing Women's
   Education (Hughes and Kennedy),
   114, 119–20
New Opportunities for Women courses
   see NOW courses
Newcastle University, 113
   Centre for Continuing Education,
      111
Newcastle upon Tyne Polytechnic,
   127
Nias, J., xiv, xvi, xvii, xviii, 10, 14, 15,
   20, 24, 65, 103
NOW courses, 111–14, 122, 127

Oakley, A., 134
observation, 36, 69, 73–5, 88–9

open-mindedness, 35–6
Open University, 'Curriculum in
    Action', 65
oppression, 137
    of women, 116, 117, 122, 128
Oxford Polytechnic, 33, 42

pairs
    of student teachers, 27–8, 38, 40
    of students, 98–9
    of tutors, 112
peer groups, xii, 38–9, 41–4, 97–9
peer leadership, 21, 28, 31
'perspective transformation', xvi, xix,
    13, 17
Peters, R. S., 64
Piaget, J., 63, 64
Pollack, S., 114, 119, 120
Pollard, A., xvi
Polyani, M., 65
Popper, K. R., 63–4
Portuges, C., 123
primary schools, xiv, 7, 15–16,
    19–32
primary teachers, 8, 14, 19, 79, 81
pupil-teacher relationships, 54–6, 60
Purvis, J., 134

quality of learning, 66, 131

rationality, 14–15, 17
reflection, xviii, xxi, 12, 33–4, 42–3,
    78, 103, 140
    resulting in change, xv, 106, 138
reflection sheets, 69, 71, 74, 77
research
    in classroom, 36, 91–106
    design, reciprocal, 132–4
    emancipatory, 133, 135, 136,
        141–2
    methodology, 127–8, 132
    process, 132, 133
    see also action research
responsibility, xvii, 35–6, 55, 59, 93,
    132
Rich, A., 129
rituals, 20, 21, 27, 30
Roberts, H., 127
Roethke, T., 90

Rogers, C., 88, 89
Rorty, R., 85
Rousseau, J. -J., 109, 128
Rowbotham, S., 121
Rudduck, J., 65, 78
Russell, T., 89
Rutenberg, T., 116, 122
Rutledge, D., 84

St Thomas Church of England
    Voluntary Aided Middle School,
    50–61
Salmon, P., 131
SCDC, 79
Schniedewind, N., 114–15
Schon, D., 14, 34–5, 65
school-college partnership, 39
school cultures, xviii–xix, 15, 25, 30,
    52, 53–4
    see also staff cultures
school development plans, 20, 21,
    49–61
    involvement of teachers, 56, 59
school experience, 23, 27–8, 31,
    38–40
Schools Curriculum Development
    Committee, 79
Schulman, L., 15–16, 17
self-esteem, 104
self-evaluation, 43, 65, 69, 78
self-image, xvi, xvii, 93, 95, 96, 97,
    104
Shor, I., 142
Showalter, E., 121
Simon, H. A., 15
skills, xv, 8–9, 31, 34, 35, 39, 40–44
    interpersonal, xiii, xviii, 22, 41
Smith, D. E., 127
'smooth running', 6
Society of Education Officers'
    Curriculum Award, 65
Somekh, B., 13–14
Spender, D., 109, 121, 127
staff cultures, 9–10, 20–21, 30, 31
    see also school cultures
staff development officers, xii, 102–3
staff meetings, 22, 51, 57
staff membership, 20–24, 31

Stanley, L., 127
strategies of support, 12, 17
Strauss, A. L., 63
student-centred learning, 96, 101, 102,
    116
student-teacher relationships, 98–100
student teachers, xiii, 19–32, 33–45,
    131–2
students, mature, 132
Sullivan, M., 3, 7–8
support, xviii
    from colleagues, 92, 106
    imposed, 3, 4–11
    mutual, xviii, 28, 112, 133
    from religion, 139
    strategies, 12, 17
support teachers, xiii, 5–6
'symbolic agreements', 7–8

Taking Liberties Collective, 116, 120
Tallantyre, F., 111
Tann, S., 41
teacher-centred classroom experience,
    96
teacher education courses, initial, xiii,
    19–45
teacher-pupil relationships, 54–6, 60
teacher-student relationships, 98–100
teaching, reflective, definition, 33–4,
    42
teaching methods, 112, 123
teaching practice see school
    experience
Teitelbaum, K., 34, 42
television, as teaching aid, 92–8
theory of education, 34–5, 63, 69
Todd, F., 97
tutors (colleges of education), xii
    role within school-based experience,
        40–41
tutors (groups)
    control, 41, 123
    role, xviii, 25, 26, 31, 36, 124–6
    skills, 25, 42, 123

tutors (NOW courses), collective
    organization, 113–14

uncertainty, 64, 67
understandings, xiii, 20, 40, 43, 44,
    83

values, xvi, xx, 42–4, 51, 69, 139,
    140
    different, 49, 52–3, 67, 112
    shared, xix, xx, 20, 21, 54, 30, 104
Vetterling-Braggin, M., 121
Vvgotsky, L. S., 64

Wagner, A. C., 15
Walker, R., 105
WEA, 113
    North Western District, 113
    Northern District, 111
Westkott, M., 116
Westminster College, 33, 38–40, 42
Whitehead, J., 65
'whole school' concept, 21, 30, 56
    curriculum planning, xiv, 28, 31
wholeheartedness, 35–6
Wilson, S. M., xix, 16
Wise, S., 127
Wolcott, H., 5
Wolverton, T., 117
women, xiii, xviii–xix, 83, 123, 133
    education, 127–9
    see also feminism
women's studies, 109–29
Woods, P., xvi, 14, 140
work patterns, 8–10
Workers' Educational Association see
    WEA
The World Yearbook of Education
    (Acker), 118–19
Wyatt, S., 51–3, 55, 59

Yeomans, R., 21

Zeichner, K. M., 15, 34, 35, 42